Rich Moran is the keenest observer of contemporary organizational life writing today, and *Trump @ Work* is Moran at his best—witty, insightful, and provocative. It is a whack-on-the-side-of-the- head book that will make you think, and question, and sometimes go crazy. You may not agree with everything that Moran says I sure didn't and he doesn't expect it—but I guarantee that reading this book will give you a whole new perspective on how leaders behave and why constituents respond the way they do.

Jim Kouzes
Coauthor of the bestselling *The Leadership Challenge*;
Executive Fellow, Center for Innovation and
Entrepreneurship, Leavey School of Business,
Santa Clara University

Rich Moran wrote the book I wish I had the courage to write. He casts a bright light on the many ways in which Trump challenges conventional management wisdom while doing things, albeit in an extreme fashion, that many other business leaders do. Just as political behavior will never be the same, so, after reading Moran's insightful book, people's ideas about leadership will be forever altered.

Jeffrey Pfeffer, Thomas D. Dee II
Professor of Organizational Behavior at Stanford University's
Graduate School of Business and author of *Leadership BS.*

T0322755

Trump @ Work points out that leadership is complex, and the actions and style of Donald Trump's do not make it any simpler. This is a book that works hard to avoid judgment while showing that Trump has us wondering about the boundaries of effective leadership. Mostly, this is an insightful look into aspects of leadership that are not often front and center, making us re-examine what really works for leaders. Whether you like Trump or not, this is a great read.

Stuart Kaplan
Leadership and Organization Advisor at Google

Leadership activities, theory, or research is not new. But sometimes, a leader comes along who defies traditional activities and assumptions. Most either love him or loathe him, but few can deny that Donald Trump challenges traditional leadership thoughts and actions. Moran brilliantly captures these 'Trumpisms' and offers new and challenging ways to lead.

Dave Ulrich, Rensis Likert Professor
Ross School of Business, University of Michigan; Partner, the RBL Group

Disruption is the word of the times and everyone wants a piece of it, including the American people. In his latest book, Moran shows that Donald Trump is disrupting widely held beliefs on leadership whether we like it or not. While Trump is disrupting leadership, Moran provides plenty of insights into what still matters.

Markos Kounalakis
McClatchy foreign affairs columnist, and author of *Trump Moves Fast and Breaks Things to Disrupt World*

Trump @ Work is not just a wake-up call, it's a slap in the face for all of us who profess to understand leadership. Don't' read this book if you don't like to be challenged, if you don't like to be uncomfortable, and if you're not willing to change. The lessons in *Trump @ Work* are now part of our knowledge base about people, management and leadership. The book shines a light on this new world order with lessons that can't be ignored, whether we like it or not.

Patty Rowland Burke
Innovation and Venture Catalyst, Center for Creative Leadership; Author, *Beating the Odds: Winning Strategies of Women in STEM*

Trump @ Work

Trump @ Work
Really Huge Lessons on
Leadership, Believe Me

Richard A. Moran

Routledge
Taylor & Francis Group

NEW YORK AND LONDON

First published 2020
by Routledge
52 Vanderbilt Avenue, New York, NY 10017

and by Routledge
2 Park Square, Milton Park, Abingdon, Oxon, OX14 4RN

Routledge is an imprint of the Taylor & Francis Group, an informa business

Library of Congress Cataloging-in-Publication Data
Names: Moran, Richard A., author.
Title: Trump @ work : really huge lessons on leadership, believe me / Richard A. Moran.
Other titles: Trump at work
Description: New York, NY : Routledge, 2020. | Includes index.
Identifiers: LCCN 2020005828 (print) | LCCN 2020005829 (ebook) | ISBN 9780367273545 (paperback) | ISBN 9780367275501 (hardback) | ISBN 9780367275495 (ebook)
Subjects: LCSH: Leadership—Moral and ethical aspects. | Management—Moral and ethical aspects. | Trump, Donald, 1946-
Classification: LCC HD57.7 .M654 2020 (print) | LCC HD57.7 (ebook) | DDC 658.4/092—dc23
LC record available at https://lccn.loc.gov/2020005828
LC ebook record available at https://lccn.loc.gov/2020005829

ISBN: 978-0-367-27550-1 (hbk)
ISBN: 978-0-367-27354-5 (pbk)
ISBN: 978-0-367-27549-5 (ebk)

Typeset in Minion
by codeMantra

Dedicated to all those who can sort through the myriad of options available and still chose to do the right thing. What matters most is what matters most.

Contents

Author xvii

Introduction.. 1
    The Trump Effect at Work.. 3
        The Things May Never Be the Same Sampler 3

Chapter 1 Credibility – Hitting a Nerve 5

    I'd Like to Believe That One… 6
    He/She Is the Only One Who Says What I've
    Been Thinking... 7
    So Were Steve Jobs and Albert Einstein 8
    What Tangled Webs We Weave............................... 9
    Sticks and Stones Can Break Your Bones.............10
    To Tell You the Truth… 11
    Where Everybody Knows Your Name................. 12
    Success Has Many Owners.................................... 13
    The Probation Period Will Be Extended 14
    Follow Me, Follow You... 15
    All Men (and Women) Are Created Equal...........16
    That's the Last Straw..16
    Think Different 17
    Objects in Rearview Mirror May Appear
    Larger than They Are..18
    When the Emperor Has No Clothes......................19
    Some Jobs Have a Very Clear Purpose 20
    Mr. Rogers or Mr. Burns? 20
    Red Baseball Cap Will Never Be the Same 21

One Small Step for Man… 21

What Part of No… 22

How to Lie with Statistics...................................... 22

And I Really Mean It This Time… 23

And One More Thing That Happened................. 23

If the Mountain Will Not Come to
Muhammed… 24

Ok, Here We Go.. 25

Kim Kardashian for President.............................. 25

Like Driving with Snow on the Windshield....... 26

Fool Me Once… 27

Chapter 2 Execution or, Just Fix It! 29

Why Do We Keep Doing This?............................. 30

It's 5:00 Somewhere 31

Even Blind Squirrels Find Acorns....................... 32

Change Is Good for Everyone, Else...................... 33

The Rule Is, There Are No Rules.......................... 34

Repotting the Plant Almost Always Means
Growth 35

I Don't Like You in That Way............................... 35

Blue Light Special Is in Aisle Four 36

Helter Skelter Is Not a Strategy… 37

Why Did It Take So Long…? 38

The Opposite of Consensus Is Dissent................. 38

When Running through Mud, Build a Bridge ... 39

That's All I Have to Say about That 40

The Lie of "Some Assembly Required"................ 41

Especially When the Stakes Are Low 41

When the Goal Posts Might Move Around........ 42

If the Only Tool You Have Is a Hammer,
Everything Is a Nail... 43

I'll Tell You When We Get There 44

Sometimes You Just Need to Start Somewhere 44

Running through the Bushes and Brambles 45

Did the Israeli Embassy Move? 46

Going to Hell but Sure Enjoying the Ride 46

Where the Rubber Meets the Sky 47

Witch Hunts and Impeachments Are
Annoying 47

Chapter 3 Communications – Can It Be Too Much? 49

Why Beat Around the Bush…? 50

Can You Hear Me Now? 51

It Was in the Middle of a Bad Day… 52

I Never Said That!… 53

Let Me Clarify What I Meant 53

The Broken Record Strategy… 54

When Emphasis Is Required! 55

Before You Hit the Send Button… 55

Good Question, Let Me Answer a Different One 56

The Trump Secret Code 56

Meet Me in Montana 57

Please Keep It in This Room 57

The Week-at-a-Glance Book Doesn't Lie 58

I Wanna Talk about Me 58

What Is Covfefe? 59

I Don't Know, but That Is What People Are
Telling Me… 59

Shaken, Not Stirred… 60

Chapter 4 Hiring and Firing Is a Blood Sport 61

Availability Is Not a Skill 62

One Bad Apple… 63

Take This Job and Shove It… 64

The Wheels Will Fall Off the Bus 65

Who Is Your Boss? 65

It Takes All Kinds of Kinds 66

I'm Not the Only One 66

Dodgeball Is Not a Fun Sport 67

Last One Out, Turn Out the Lights 67

The Hatchet Man Cometh… 68

Test Drives Are Free 68

Take the Hill, Please 69

Chapter 5 About the Critics – Can They All Be
Wrong? 71

If You Don't Like My Twang 72

I Looked under the Covers… 72

But It Just May Be a Lunatic You're Looking
For… 73

When Everyone Is above Average 73

Bad Situations Can Always Turn Worse 74

Get Them before They Get You 74

Uh, Oh 75

Beware of the Circular Firing Squad 75

A Bulletproof Vest Can Be a
Fashion Accessory 76

How Can They Be Sure? 76

They Can't All Be Wrong. Or Can They? 77

Only the Paranoid Survive 77

And Never, Ever Read the Comments 78

Chapter 6 Is Loyalty Just a Four-Letter Word? 79

You Have the Right to Remain Silent… 80

Now Is My Chance… 81

Act Like You Love Me 82

Will Your Lawyer Talk to God for You? 83

What Were Once Memories Are Now Evidence.....84

Let It Go, Let It Flow 85

The Wingman Cometh 86

I Am Going to Count to Three… 87

I Smell a Rat... 88

Chapter 7 Being Current and Doing Homework........... 89

Measure Twice, Cut Once… 90

When You Stop Learning, You Die...................... 90

Comes from a Long Line 91

There's Your Trouble 92

Where Is That Remote?.. 92

Toga! Toga! Toga!.. 93

It's Hard to Keep Up... 94

Based on a True Story 95

Happy Days Are Here Again................................. 96

Runs Great, Needs Engine..................................... 97

Read All about It… 97

Think Anyone Will Notice? 98

Chapter 8 Judgment Is in the Eye of the Beholder 99

Some of My Best Friends… 100

No Gray Area Exists.. 100

What, Are You in the Third Grade...? 101

One Man's Ceiling Is Another Man's Floor 101

This Could Be a Problem… 102

All I Do Is Win… 102

God, Country, Apple Pie 103

Sink or Swim Management Can Lead to
Great Things.. 104

If I Shot You When I Wanted, I'd Be Out
by Now 104

I Love the Smell of a "Sharpie" in
the Morning 105

I Didn't Know You Could Speak Latin 105

Never Waste a Crisis 106

Never Going Back to My Old School 107

Cheeseburger in Paradise 108

Plagues, Locusts, Floods, Fifty Car Pileups 109

Sorry Seems to Be the Hardest Word 109

Shiny Objects and Butterflies Are Always
Flying Around 110

Look at It This Way… 110

It Really Isn't Over until It's Over 111

Second Opinion Not Required 111

At Least We're All Wrong Together 112

I Used to Be Somebody, Now I Am
Somebody Else 113

All the King's Horses and All the King's Men ... 114

Receiving a Subpoena Usually Means You
Need to Show Up 115

Is This My Last Chance? 115

Who Doesn't Love a Parade? 116

Someday, Just Not Today 116

It Was Just Playing Around 117

Chapter 9 Not Quite Right (NQR) – Really? 119

I Hear You Knocking but I'm Not Here 120

Hindsight Can Be Blurry 121

Its Only Four Years… 122

The "Permanent Record" Does Exist 123

You Can't Make This Stuff Up 124

It Worked in the Lab 125
Hell Hath No Fury… 126
Since I Won the Lottery, I Have New Friends.... 127
Are Iceland or Belgium Available? 128
Terms Are Thirty Days 129
Being on Constant "Red Alert" Status Is
Good Defense but Exhausting 130
Sometimes It Is Rocket Science 131
In Case of Emergency, Break Glass 132
You Need to Calm Down 133
I Didn't Do Anything Wrong 134
Sitting Down Is the New Smoking 135
You Don't Pull the Mask Off the Old Lone
Ranger 136
How Do You Like Me Now? 137
Now What? 137

Chapter 10 Personal Traits, Habits, Ticks,
                  and Quirks 139

When the Dog Catches the Car 140
The Mirror Doesn't Lie 141
Look for the Bare Necessities 141
Do You Hear What I Hear? 142
Smile Like You Mean It 142
Is Mine Bigger Than Yours? 143
Storming Out of Meetings Will Always
Make for Short Meetings 143
He May Be an Asshole but He's Our Asshole ... 144
You Probably Think This Is All about You 144
Smuckers, Forbes, Kohler, Ford 145
I Am Not Racist But… 145
When I Was Your Age 146

I Am Exhausted 147

It's Difficult to Travel with Golf Clubs............... 148

That Was Your First Mistake................................149

Your Mother Wears Combat Boots.................... 150

What's Wrong with You? How Stupid Can
You Be? 150

Not Everyone Can Dance with the Stars............151

If I Only Knew Then What I Know Now 152

Management Is Not Like a Box of Chocolates...153

What's Someone Like You Doing in a Place
Like This? 154

The Best Thing about Golf Is a Mulligan 155

Because You've Got to Have Friends.................. 155

What Goes Around Really Does Come
Around 156

If You Don't Know a Bully, You Are One.......... 156

What Did Mother Teresa Really Do Anyway?.... 157

Unless You Are Tiger Woods............................... 157

Flattery Can Get You Everywhere....................... 158

Future's so Bright I Need My Shades 159

Mirror, Mirror on the Wall 159

A White Sports Coat and a Pink Carnation..... 160

Chapter 11 Making Deals Is an Art, a Science, and a
Mystery 161

Answer Hazy, Try Again… 162

All or Nothing Usually Means Nothing.............162

Hoisting the Distress Flags..................................163

Gray Is the New Black… 163

Are You with Me or Against Me?....................... 164

You Can't Always Get What You Want............. 164

It's All about the Benjamin's 165

Chapter 12 The Summary... 167

    Old Dogs and New Tricks Give a Clue 167
    Unprecedented. That's IT. That's All… 168

Epilogue.. 169

Index... 171

Author

Richard A. Moran is an investor, author, and an evangelist for organizational effectiveness. He has authored eight best-selling books and is credited with starting the genre of *"Business Bullet* Books" with *Never Confuse a Memo with Reality.* He is a frequent speaker on workplace issues and hosts a syndicated weekend radio show on CBS called *In the Workplace.*

PREVIOUS BOOKS BY RICHARD A. MORAN

Never Confuse a Memo with Reality
Beware Those Who Ask for Feedback
Cancel the Meetings, Keep the Doughnuts
Fear No Yellow Stickies
Nuts Bolts and Jolts
Navigating Tweets, Feats and Deletes
Sins and CEOs
The Thing about Work

Introduction

I didn't want to write a book about Donald Trump. There are lots of those already. And besides, his style and actions are too polarizing. But then it occurred to me, he is changing the way the work world operates and that is my territory. It's hard enough to keep up with leadership and management trends. Donald Trump is making it more difficult, not intentionally, not through the tweets he writes, but by how he is challenging the long existing norms. Who knew that tweeting would become an established way of communicating to an organization? Who knew that in spite of constant searing criticism, one could disregard it and continue to follow an agenda? Who knew that preaching to supporters and ignoring naysayers is a way to manage?

"I hate Donald Trump" is not the message intended in these pages although you will gather my opinions about some of his actions. I don't know Donald Trump and have never met him. Whether you like Donald Trump or not, he has had an impact on the thinking about leadership and management. In these pages I try to neither support nor condemn Donald Trump although at times it is difficult to not take a position. I am only trying to explore the changes he has wrought at work.

Unprecedented is the word that is most often associated with Donald Trump. Unprecedented when it comes to Mr. Trump means "never before" or "this has never been done before". But when it comes to Trump, other thoughts are associated with "unprecedented". Those thoughts include the following:

- I can't believe he did that...
- Will he get away with that?

- Maybe we should have been doing it this all along.
- No one else speaks the truth like him.
- He lies and gets away with it, can I do that?

The behavior of Mr. Trump is easy to dismiss but it should not be. For better or worse, he has redefined the Presidency and in so doing, challenged thoughts on leadership and management. He has redefined background checks and transparency. Imagine just a few years ago a President who has been divorced twice, who is not a churchgoer, who will not turn over tax reports, and who refuses to ever apologize getting elected President.

Agree with him or not, Trump has changed things.

"Appropriate behavior" is a phrase that comes up in all leadership rules of engagement. That is, it is the duty of any leader to only engage in appropriate behavior. The question now is: What is appropriate behavior? And it's not only the actions of Donald Trump that is bringing this rhetorical question to the fore.

For example, in Canada or certain states where Cannabis is legal, is smoking pot appropriate behavior for a leader? Is a tweet in which the appearance of another is mocked OK? What about speaking to a controversial group that preaches hate or remaining silent on abhorrent behavior?

The rules are changing, and Trump is accelerating the change. Not in the way you might be asking. Probably no need to change your behavior tomorrow. Your style and tactics may not change but I hope to give you pause, to think about things differently, consider other angles, and provoke a few thoughts. At least a few anecdotes to consider at your next staff meetings like, "do we really need consensus?"

Depending upon your political leaning, you may love some entries and be put off by others. Both are good outcomes as my intent is to invoke new thinking by observing a leader who is doing things in unconventional ways.

Maybe all of those leadership theories were wrong. Maybe credibility doesn't matter for a leader. Maybe popularity doesn't matter as much as some accomplishments. Maybe morals are changing, and some things just don't matter as much.

As a student of leadership and management, I have followed Trump, sometimes with horror and sometimes with wonder. Amidst all the noise, he is changing things, so let's take a look. Believe me.

THE TRUMP EFFECT AT WORK

The Things May Never Be the Same Sampler

- Twitter is an accepted internal communications vehicle. All day every day.
- Reaching consensus is an option, not a requirement. Autocratic decisions are efficient.
- Don't waste time trying to win the non-supporters over. Stick with the rabid supporters.
- Meetings can be ended if the leader walks out.
- Standards change. No need to be embarrassed about divorces or hanging out with adult film stars.
- Political correctness is an option. Tolerance to others and other's points of view is optional.
- No apology is ever necessary.
- Never discuss politics to those who disagree with you. There is no middle.

1

Credibility – Hitting a Nerve

The one trait that is most often associated with leaders is credibility. All the literature about management effectiveness points right at credibility. When it comes to Donald Trump, credible is not an adjective often connected to him. Yet, he doesn't apologize, correct, or explain and for that he is both reviled and celebrated. Too bad leaders are not equipped with a Pinocchio nose that could help identify the size of any fibbing. Is it ok to fib to advance a career? Is it ok to fib to advance the organization's mission? The verdict is mixed but ask anyone, credibility still matters. We want to believe our leaders and not question what is true.

I'D LIKE TO BELIEVE THAT ONE...

- *Credibility might be all that matters in the long run for a leader to be successful.*

When a leader's credibility is in question, the leader is in trouble. A leader needs to be able to communicate ideas and strategies and solutions without others wondering if the truth is being told or if there is logic behind the thinking. A falsehood will crush credibility right away. A series of lies will allow thoughts of the leader to wander into "unfit" territory. It may be appropriate from time to time to tell a fib for the good of the organization but credibility needs to be restored. Lying is the enemy of credibility. Overcoming a lack of credibility is a high hurdle to clear once credibility is questioned. Better to start with gaining credibility and trust and in so doing, building support.

HE/SHE IS THE ONLY ONE WHO SAYS WHAT I'VE BEEN THINKING

- *Telling people what they want to hear will ensure supporters but may box you in to a corner from which you may not be able to escape.*

We have all heard someone say, "Finally, someone is saying what I have been thinking for years" implying that others never knew what they were thinking. Maybe. Telling it like it is does not mean it's accurate. Telling it like it is doesn't make it right. Is it the truth or just playing to a bias? Credibility includes the truth, judgment, the message, and perspective. It does not mean pandering to what people want to hear. And not everyone wants to hear the same thing. Building a message on what people are thinking but has not been declared can work, if it's the truth. Donald Trump built a campaign on expressing what others are only thinking. It got him elected.

SO WERE STEVE JOBS AND ALBERT EINSTEIN

- *"Unprecedented" can be a complement when applied to big actions.*

The word "unprecedented" could mean much more than "this is the first time". It could mean this is the breakthrough that the world has long awaited. It could also mean "WTF!" Leaders need to break molds and kill sacred cows as well as keep adversaries on their heels. Whether it be meeting with "sort of" enemies, visiting forbidden lands, or breaking long-established protocols, Donald Trump is the master of the unprecedented. He has tread where no President has ever gone before and considers those groundbreaking steps to be what a leader does. So do his followers. When change is required, "unprecedented" may be required.

WHAT TANGLED WEBS WE WEAVE

- *Truth does prevail. Any lies, fibs, and other falsehoods may be glossed over in the short term but can come back to haunt you.*

Life is easier when you don't have to try to remember what you said. It is often the case that lying about something that happened will get you in more trouble than the thing you might lie about. (See Richard Nixon, Bill Clinton.) Most of us have the ambition to keep life simple. Telling the truth just makes life easier. More importantly, if you lie, you get caught. The million dollars a year salaried executive who lies on an expense report and is fired will testify to that principle. If you find it hard to sleep when you are worried about what might be found out later, you are living a life that does not feature credibility as a foundation. Any misstatements of Donald Trump are out there, but the world is going so fast that there is no going back for corrections. No haunting yet or maybe ever.

STICKS AND STONES CAN BREAK YOUR BONES

- *Responding to critics can be counterproductive and a waste of time. Recognize at some point that the critics may be right.*

Critics are always out there. A leader who is not being criticized is not doing much. Regardless of any decision a leader makes, some will not like it. The more controversial the decision, the more the critics will howl. Responding to every criticism is a time suck that is infinite and probably does not appease any critic. Better to pay some attention to the criticism and make changes as necessary but don't be consumed by critics. Recognize, however, that if the howls last long enough and are loud enough, the critics might be right, and a change is required. Or, like Donald Trump, ignore the critics or get even, there is no middle.

TO TELL YOU THE TRUTH...

- *Trusting your team is as important as the expertise of the team.*

A leader who is not trusted will fail. A leader who doesn't trust the rest of his or her team will fail because the important work will not be delegated. Trust should go deep. Trust is not just about lying or stealing or about keeping secrets. Trust too is about competency and letting people do their jobs. Trust is about valuing other people's opinions. Trust is about doing what you say you will do. Trust is about believing those around you are not secretly keeping notes for a book. Effective leaders surround themselves with people that can be trusted both ethically and from a competency perspective. If the team is only one, yourself, then things are a lot easier. No need to take votes or discuss issues. Donald Trump often operates with that team of one. It may be efficient but opinion is very mixed about how effective that party of one operates.

WHERE EVERYBODY KNOWS YOUR NAME

- *Remember that the "Person of the Year" has included some bad hombres.*

The most famous person in the world is just that, famous. Homer Simpson is famous around the world. So are Korean Boy Bands. Adolph Hitler was *Time* Magazine Man of the Year in 1938 and infamous. Are they leaders? Most would argue not but they are famous. Donald Trump is the most famous person in the world right now and that means that his dream may be fulfilled but does not mean that his leadership style is embraced or admired. Leaders command attention based on the position held and as a result become a brand. The brand should be used to push a positive agenda. When the leader holds the platform something should be done that will make the place better, whatever that place may be.

SUCCESS HAS MANY OWNERS

- *When the measures that people care about are looking good take credit, even if outstanding performance has nothing to do with you. Sometimes throw in the caveat that maybe others helped or that you inherited the situation.*

People care about their own welfare and, to a lesser extent, the welfare of those around them which means they pay attention to the economy in general. People care about and want good news like job growth or improving wages or getting the "bad guy" or diplomatic victories. For a leader, when good things happen, take credit and be unabashedly proud of the accomplishments. Giving some credit to previous leaders will make any leader look generous. Sharing the credit, if possible, is better than to just taking credit. Throwing others under the bus so that you can look good will always lead to trouble ahead. The "others" who went under the bus will find ways, sometimes subtle, so that next time there will be no credit to take. The economy goes up and down. Blaming others for it going down and claiming credit for any uptick is not credible.

THE PROBATION PERIOD WILL BE EXTENDED

- *Performance reviews happen every day because any leader is so visible. There are no days off.*

Leaders don't get mental health days. Leaders don't look forward to "snow days". In fact, leaders don't and can't get sick. If the President or a CEO wants to call in sick, who does he or she call? Leaders are always "on" whether it be in an office, on a podium, in an airplane, at a dinner, or on the golf course. Performance is as much a perception as a reality, and the perception of how one performs day to day can change. A hero one week can be the asshole the next week. The sense that the leader is getting things done is the variable that will effect that perception. Donald Trump has polished the perception that he is getting things done. Whether what he is getting done is good or bad is up for debate and in the eye of the beholder.

FOLLOW ME, FOLLOW YOU

- *The number of followers you have on social media does not reflect people who agree with you. Some will follow just to roll their eyes at what you post. Social media does not define you.*

Think of the laughing babies, the grandmothers reading books, piano playing cats, and Duck Dynasty actors pitching cleaning products. They all have a lot of followers and so do lots of other people. It's a badge like the number of Frequent Flyer Miles you can collect. Followers matter but the numbers can be misleading. Your followers may be laughing at you, they may be copying you, they may be cheering for you but they don't define you. In many cases, followers are like gawkers looking at an accident on the highway – they are curious and may or may not help you.

ALL MEN (AND WOMEN) ARE CREATED EQUAL

- *Never mock the disabled or anyone that seems at a disadvantage. It creates the bully image that never goes away.*

I am not quite sure why I need to mention this one. Cruelty might be the worst of any traits I can think of in a leader or any individual for that matter. Sensitivity and empathy are more akin to the traits that people look for in a leader and what we should aspire to. A leader who ignores this truth does so at his or her own peril of being removed as a leader. Better to be known as the inclusive, compassionate leader than any alternative descriptor. For Donald Trump, clues abound as to whether he is a sensitive person or a tough bully. You make the decision.

THAT'S THE LAST STRAW

- *Know at what point your most ardent supporters will abandon you.*

We all have our limits. I liked Lance Armstrong for a long time until I learned he had been cheating for so long. I liked Kevin Spacey and lots of others too until I learned more details about them. Supporters love leaders for certain characteristics like the belief that they get things done or that they say things that I think or they stand up to others. But for any leader, those same supporters have a limit and can turn the other way based on any sign of change or weakness. Know what that limit is even if it is hypothetical like "shooting someone on 5th Avenue".

THINK DIFFERENT

- *Slogans and tag lines can be helpful but can come back to haunt you.*

"Lock her up" is not an uplifting positive message that leaders want to convey. Neither is "send them back", and leadership is about redirecting those types of messages into more positive ones like "Make America Great Again". Recognize that the most successful slogans in the corporate world are about hope, aspirations, or creativity or something special, not about vindictiveness or being mean. A tag line can emerge when you may not want it to and can be tough to kill. Doing nothing will be a sign of encouragement and support and will be used against a leader, no matter. Clarity about being supportive or not tolerating certain behaviors is important. Ambiguity implies support.

OBJECTS IN REARVIEW MIRROR MAY APPEAR LARGER THAN THEY ARE

- *Making anything "great" again is hopeful and nostalgic at the same time.*

BUT, sometimes the way it used to be only looks good in hindsight. We remember things better than they actually were. The spirit of "Make America Great Again" harkens back to a time when life was more simple and clear and John Wayne ruled the world. The slogan also intimates a time when there were fewer immigrants and prejudice was tolerated among a slew of other bad things. Leaders look forward not backward. There is no way to go back anyway so a leader might conjure up renewal or change for the better, not going backward. Leaders look ahead to a better state and make others believe in that future state. Not "the way we were".

WHEN THE EMPEROR HAS NO CLOTHES

* *Telling the truth is more than telling the truth.*

The truth too is acknowledging what is going on around you, good and bad. A mass shooting with a terrible loss of life and a self-proclaimed white supremacist as the alleged shooter is nothing more than an act of terrorism. A leader tells the truth about such a horrific event, labels it what it is, and promises to do something about it. Then does something about it. To not do anything about it is just one more empty promise that will erode credibility especially when such terrible acts continue to happen. A leader who is proud of a record of accomplishments can build on that record and the inherent credibility to do more, to take more action. When bad things happen and time after time, the leader makes empty promises, the leader will finally be seen as having no clothes.

SOME JOBS HAVE A VERY CLEAR PURPOSE

- *The job of a fact checker is to check facts.*

Nitpickers are a simple animal designed to pick nits. Fact checkers are a close cousin; their job is to check facts. Given the access that the Internet provides, facts are reasonably easy to check. Once checked, the facts are hard to deny although it is still possible. When hyperbole, criticisms, name-calling, and half-truths are combined with checked facts, what results is a babble of words that can sometimes actually be believed. Donald Trump has mastered the expression of word soup that can have people wondering what he just said but believing it might be correct, regardless of the fact checkers.

MR. ROGERS OR MR. BURNS?

- *A leader's nickname says a lot about how that leader is perceived. Pay attention.*

Who doesn't like Mr. Rogers? Everyone likes him. No one likes Mr. Burns from *The Simpsons* TV show fame. Which will it be? They are both leaders and I am sure there are bosses out there with each of those nicknames. One nickname is welcome more than the other. Behaviors are what dictate any labels. How a leader acts comes back in many ways including nicknames. Mr. Trump has many nicknames, but none have really stuck. In fact, lots of things have not stuck to him to his credit. Our President Trump, a name that sounds almost royal, is more likely to give a nickname than be nicknamed.

RED BASEBALL CAP WILL NEVER BE THE SAME

- *Symbols that take on negative connotations reflect on the leader who introduced that symbol.*

The list of offensive symbols does not need to be reviewed. Many of those symbols that started long ago are still around and were either created or endorsed by a leader. The same holds for symbols that we love. Leaders have the power to create symbols. For Donald Trump, that red baseball cap with the phrase "Make America Great Again" is his and only his. Whether that cap becomes the symbol of a strong leader and his accomplishments or a symbol of bigotry and divisiveness is a question that is yet to be answered. In the meantime, be careful with that cap in certain circles.

ONE SMALL STEP FOR MAN...

- *Some comments are just too memorable and will always be part of the brand.*

Among other things, a leader's legacy is a phrase or comment that resonates with the time, the style, and what people hear. Think of Kennedy's "Ask not what your country can do for you…" or Nixon's "I am not a crook". The quote "I could shoot somebody in the middle of 5th Avenue and not lose any voters" is one that will stick too. It could be true, and it could be a sign of a brand with infinite loyalty or it could be a statement of hubris. Leaders need to choose words carefully; words stick with the persona for a long time.

WHAT PART OF NO...

- *Some decisions are never worth revisiting.*

Leaders know how to say no. Leaders look at data, talk to people, and look at options, then the leader makes a decision. Sometimes the answer is no. Sometimes saying no is not popular. Once the decision is made, others will pester and bicker and nag in the hopes of looking at that decision once again and converting the NO to a yes or at least a maybe. Donald Trump is a world-class expert on saying no and not revisiting the decision. It irritates his detractors, but while further discussions are being held, he has moved on. Making a decision and sticking with it is a leadership skill.

HOW TO LIE WITH STATISTICS

- *Be sure of statistics and data, the right ones are always helpful.*

If unsure, couch any statements in the phrase "based on what others are telling me". In so doing, you can avoid the phrase "I stand corrected". Any good statistician recognizes that the numbers can swing in lots of different ways. Leaders understand which numbers are important and which ones others will pay attention to. Unemployment is a number that will always be front and center. The national debt number is so large that very few understand it. Like the President, pick all the numbers that will make you look good.

AND I REALLY MEAN IT THIS TIME...

- *Saying "Believe Me!" doesn't make anything more believable.*

"To tell you the truth" is usually just a placeholder, but it can be a phrase that implies "I am breaking new ground and telling you something that has not been the case before". Then, sometimes the truth is not told. It's like trying to underline what was just said as if that is the true part. Figures of speech and colloquial phrases that emphasize the truth do not help anything become more true. If the truth is told, there doesn't need to be any qualifiers, asterisks, or exclamation points.

AND ONE MORE THING THAT HAPPENED

- *Complaining is not a trait admired in a leader.*

No one wants to be around whiners. Coffee cups in every office in the world declare "No Whiners". Whining is not just how you might think of the office crank who complains about the lack of snacks in the break room every day. Whining from a leader can be much more subtle. Whining can be about the media or the polls or the lack of honest reporting or the referees at the game or the meter maids who issued a ticket or the inaccurate count of spectators at an event. It doesn't matter what the subject is about. Whining from a leader sounds like that leader cannot solve problems.

IF THE MOUNTAIN WILL NOT
COME TO MUHAMMED...

- *Visiting hostile territory may not be fun, but it can show bravery and a willingness to listen. That is, if you are willing to listen.*

Some situations and people are intractable and prove it over long periods of time. To make things happen and break the frozen chain, sometimes leaders need to meet others half way. To do otherwise is to stay stuck in a situation that will never change. Sometimes the implications are more complicated than they may appear and experts in policy and negotiations need to be involved. President Trump has taken risks, some would say, broken glass to change the status quo. In some cases, he lived up to the motto, "If it ain't broke, break it".

OK, HERE WE GO

- *Sometimes it's best to take a deep breath and start all over by telling the truth.*

Lies, fibs, exaggerations, and untruths tend to make the difficult role of leadership even more difficult. One fib leads to others creating a knot that only gets worse. Going back to where it all started and correcting the story is the best way to be released from the trap of fibs. The outcome may be better than you expected. The old bromide about the truth being easier to remember especially applies to leaders. For any President, the fact checkers and journalists that check on the truth are everywhere and will challenge any untruth. May as well start with the truth.

KIM KARDASHIAN FOR PRESIDENT

- *Being a celebrity and being competent are not the same thing.*

People gain fame and become household names for all kinds of reasons. Celebrity and skills are not the same thing. Leaders want and need to be known. A healthy ego is a big part of the process that propels people into leadership roles so by definition there is a celebrity element to leadership. Leaders can become celebrities and use that celebrity to be more effective. Celebrities can become leaders, but unless something in their background prepared them to be leaders, it will be a struggle. Reality television to most powerful person in the world is a stretch.

LIKE DRIVING WITH SNOW ON THE WINDSHIELD

- *The difference between not caring and not knowing doesn't matter.*

Chicken or egg? We like both breakfast as well as chicken nuggets so who cares? When it comes to whether our leaders are clueless or just don't care, the same can be said, who cares? It is a bad trait in either case. When a leader doesn't do homework, doesn't listen at briefings, doesn't attend meetings, or doesn't solicit advice from the experts, that leader is going to make mistakes. When a leader broadcasts an attitude of not caring about the less privileged or not caring about people in other parts of the world, that leader is going to make mistakes too. The mistakes matter, but it doesn't matter whether they are based on being naïve or cruel.

FOOL ME ONCE...

- *A leader almost always starts out with the confidence of followers and the belief among them that the truth will be told. It is a sacred trust not to be broken.*

The benefit of the doubt is a gift given to leaders on a silver platter by followers. It is not a gift that should be taken lightly. Even when there are reasons to doubt credibility, we want to believe in the leader and his or her judgment to do the right thing. But there is a limit. Once there is so much evidence that the leader is not being forthright that we no longer believe, the leader will not gain that credibility back. Each of us has a different threshold on believing in a leader. For some, credibility will be lost on the first fib. For others, a willingness to accept lies from leaders is nearly limitless as long as there is a sense that the leader is taking actions in their best interest. It can boggle the mind what some are willing to accept.

2

Execution or, Just Fix It!

Donald Trump was elected because voters believed he would get things done. He was a no-nonsense guy. It would not be gridlock as usual. And the belief among many is that he **is** getting things done. Whether or not we agree with what he is getting done is another question. He is getting some of the bad guys. He is eliminating regulations. He is signing executive orders. He is citing statistics and taking credit for a strong economy. People love a leader who they believe is making things happen. In spite of the morass of issues and controversies that any leader might create, getting things done is still the currency that will endow a leader with followers.

WHY DO WE KEEP DOING THIS?

- *Always ask the questions "Why do we keep doing it this way or why are we doing this at all?"*

We get stuck. Inertia is the enemy of all things innovative. Sometimes we don't know why we are doing things this way? Why do we need to fill all these jobs? Why did we create this process? Organizations do get stuck and the change agent needs to be relentless in going after the same old same old. Sometimes how you ask is as important as what you ask. "Visible signs of progress" (VSOP) means things are changing, and the fastest way to show VSOP is to stop doing things that people hate. The actions could be eliminating onerous regulations or antiquated processes or any irritating requirement. Cheers will ensue. Trump built a platform on eliminating swamps and regulations and making a return to more simple times. Leaders can learn from his VSOP approach.

IT'S 5:00 SOMEWHERE

• *Doing nothing is sometimes better than doing anything.*

"Just sit there!" It would be nice if the words of your mother applied to leaders, but they don't. Leaders have no choice, even if they just want to watch television all day, things happen, decisions need to be made, problems need to be addressed, documents need to be signed, and everything else. It's not only about the buck stopping; it's about moving forward, even a little bit. Even if we want a leader to do nothing, it is almost impossible. Some believed Mr. Trump would do nothing based on his lack of experience. To the chagrin of many, it is no longer possible to be a do-nothing leader. All leaders are always running for reelection or a new contract here are too many means to check performance. Trump is no exception.

EVEN BLIND SQUIRRELS FIND ACORNS

- *Trying to accomplish a thousand things at once may lead to lucky success.*

Fighting impeachment while dealing with Israeli issues followed by an Iran Treaty crisis followed by dealing with interest rates going up followed by tweeting about immigration followed by trying to buy another country followed by weighing in on Brexit is all consuming and it's now almost time for lunch. Leadership can be exhausting with so much to do. Trying to plan is nearly impossible since there is so much reacting to do on any given day. Since planning is so difficult, keeping everyone off balance by the huge volume of initiatives started can actually get things done in the right direction. It may not be pretty, but sometimes any activity is better than waiting. As Trump knows, continuous actions and deflections will make supporters and others wonder what is happening today rather than fixing what happened yesterday. Getting impeached? Let's go to Davos.

CHANGE IS GOOD FOR EVERYONE, ELSE

- *Given the option, people will almost always reject "As Is". Other change options are appealing until they affect you.*

No one seems to like the "as is" state and wants to change. But does that mean going back to the way it was when we were "great" or does it mean going forward into places that might be riskier. Going back is really never an option, and it was probably not as great as we remember anyway. But there is a certain romance to those good old days. All organizations need to change, the definition of what the change entails is what matters. The person who can best define the change is often going to be the leader. Donald Trump straddles the paradox of let's change things and let's return America to greatness. It works for his supporters.

THE RULE IS, THERE ARE NO RULES

- *Simplifying or eliminating regulations can remove burdens and be welcome.*

Too many rules and regulations slow things down, no doubt. But most rules and regulations were put in place for a reason whether it be to protect something or someone or to deter bad behavior. Sometimes those rules and regulations run their course and there is no need for them. Those are the ones to be eliminated and rejoicing should ensue. Others need to be kept in place and as onerous as they may seem, the reason they were enacted is still good, depending on who you talk to. The wholesale elimination of regulations without thought is dangerous. Donald Trump's plan to "let's start all over and then see what we need" is playing with fire. Literally.

REPOTTING THE PLANT ALMOST ALWAYS MEANS GROWTH

- *Reinventing yourself can take many turns, so embrace the journey.*

Real estate mogul, billionaire playboy, reality show star, President of the United States, now that is reinvention, especially at an older age. Good for anyone who can perform such big time reinventing. Donald Trump and his reinvention activities could be a model for AARP. Inherent in reinvention is the experience factor. That is, bringing some experience from a previous life into the new one and then learning and thriving in the new environment. The reinvention is there, the thriving is there, the learning is there, the effectiveness is still a question. But he is repotted.

I DON'T LIKE YOU IN THAT WAY

- *Being likable is not as important as getting things done.*

The best teacher, regardless of the subject, is one who is demanding, and you may hate that teacher from time to time but you learn. The best teachers and some would say the best leaders don't care about "likability". But the "likability index" is always something that politicians always pay attention to – until Donald Trump. The likability surveys for Donald Trump are always at or near record lows for a President. In spite of the fact that most people don't like him, many more support him because they believe he is doing a good job by getting things done. Results matter more than a smile or winning personality.

BLUE LIGHT SPECIAL IS IN AISLE FOUR

- *Bring attention only to those things that you want to highlight. Let other things go if you can.*

Focus, focus, focus, that's what leadership is all about. It's impossible. The thinking is that if you focus, things will get done and the rest of the world will be inspired and follow. But sometimes leaders are their own worst enemy and get unfocused and work on too many initiatives. Lots of "shiny objects" will be presented to any leader and many are worth doing but bandwidth is only so wide. Even suggestions and exploratory questions can take a leader offtrack. Don't be your own worst enemy and say, "Why did I bring that up?" For a leader, some subjects are like a Pandora's box, once the subject is broached, there is no return and others will seize the opportunity to go in another direction. Choose the right area in which to focus. Mr. Trump likes those shiny objects.

HELTER SKELTER IS NOT A STRATEGY...

- *It is difficult to be effective when distractions are bombarding you at every turn and others nitpick every single thing you do.*

Ever tried to work on something important when you are constantly interrupted? Ever tried to be productive when you are facing constant criticism and hysteria all around. It's nearly impossible. The pings and pangs of texts and emails when trying to concentrate can drive us all crazy. For a leader, the bombardment of distractions never ends and can make a huge difference in effectiveness. When working on nuclear disarmament treaties, imagine how hard it is to concentrate when there is a threat that your children might be indicted. Hard to imagine, but the elimination of distractions is a must for a leader to be successful. Just imagine the distractions that face Donald Trump each day. Just watch the news.

WHY DID IT TAKE SO LONG...?

- *Solving a long-standing or pent-up problem will assure big approval ratings. Find the intractable irritations and make changes or innovate to fix them.*

Think appointments at the DMV or wheels on suitcases or electric outlets at airports or meal delivery services. All of these simple ideas made our lives better. Some processes and problems and solutions seem like they are so much a part of the culture that when they are fixed, hero worship ensues. Likewise, the acceleration of drug approvals that might help the terminally ill or expanding benefits for veteran could be worthy of an accolade. Every organization has a set of problems that seem unsolvable, but fixing them will earn gold stars and garner supporters. The elimination of some onerous banking regulations and rebuilding the military are areas where Donald Trump scored points as a leader.

THE OPPOSITE OF CONSENSUS IS DISSENT

- *Consensus is worth the effort.*

Some say consensus is when everyone agrees to do something that no one wants to do. Others say that without consensus any decision will be torpedoed by those who don't agree. An impatient leader won't be very interested in consensus. Consensus takes meetings and time. Without consensus, things might get done and it all may work out, but there could be dead bodies along the way. Consensus and Trump are rarely used in the same sentence. How about never?

WHEN RUNNING THROUGH MUD, BUILD A BRIDGE

- *Lots of little progress might add up to change in the long run, but for a leader, big things matter.*

Executive orders are useful since they bypass lots of bureaucracy. Eliminating annoying regulations can show that you recognize them and are not afraid to change them. Withdrawing from meaningless treaties and agreements is fine and dandy. For any leader, lots of small decisions present themselves each day and can take up each day. At the end of the proverbial day, the leader can with confidence say, "I got a lot done today". Not quite. Leaders are charged with doing big things, making big decisions, and striking bold moves, and all those small moves are not enough. Every day takes all day. Find the big things or the bureaucracy that you are probably trying to eliminate will consume you. To drain the swamp is more complicated than pulling one plug. As the song says, maybe a little less talk, a lot more action is required.

THAT'S ALL I HAVE TO SAY ABOUT THAT

- *Command and control management is not dead. Turns out some people like it.*

The top-down management style was pronounced dead long ago. Even the military changed its ways to accommodate a more inclusive management style. What was more important than giving orders was employee engagement. Empowerment was the way to make organizations successful and ensure that everyone lived happily ever after. Building teams is the key to success or at least that's what experts in management believed. Workshops prevailed with sticky notes all over the walls detailing how important it is that all voices be heard. Not so fast. Turns out lots of people want a leader who operates without a lot of input from others and tells people what to do. And we know one who operates that way.

THE LIE OF "SOME ASSEMBLY REQUIRED"

- *Reading the instructions is always a step in the right direction.*

Complex issues almost never have simple solutions. Sophisticated events require planning and more planning. Large operations of people or equipment require logistics that are complicated and should not be underestimated. Leaders don't need to pay attention to every detail, but they do need to understand the complexity of situations and bring resources to bear that will make the complex seem simple. However, having some grasp of the details will make any leader look more competent. Donald Trump doesn't read the manuals and believes his "gut instincts" will guide him through the most complex issues. We hope so.

ESPECIALLY WHEN THE STAKES ARE LOW

- *Politics can convert a short meeting into a long one with no result.*

Results matter. Meetings don't matter. No one was ever reelected on the number of meetings attended, and Donald Trump understands this better than anyone. Any political organization is ripe with meetings and more meetings, but if nothing is getting accomplished, why meet? There is an old joke: "Why are universities so political?" Answer: "Because the stakes are so low". When it comes to meetings and politics, it is a deadly combination that can hurt a leader. Trump knows.

WHEN THE GOAL POSTS MIGHT MOVE AROUND

- *Know at what point your most ardent supporters will abandon you.*

Leaders move goal posts all the time. Sometimes conditions change and the variables that effect the location of goal posts means they move. Knowing when to move them is a skill that leaders develop over time and to their own advantage. Deadlines for tariff discussion with China move every day. Thresholds for environmental safety rules move based on weather and perceptions of climate change. Mr. Trump is the master at manipulating goal posts to demonstrate leadership.

IF THE ONLY TOOL YOU HAVE IS A HAMMER, EVERYTHING IS A NAIL

- *Try something new when confronted with a history of failures.*

After a while, constant harassing, intimidation, and bullying will wear others down and others will just cave in with a sigh of resignation. Doing nothing or a constant diet of saying "NO" can change the behavior of others as well. They just give up. Wearing down others or doing nothing can be a strategy but neither will move any organization forward. The leader's toolbox needs to have lots of other skills like diplomacy, empathy, communications and more. A leader also needs to be credible, confident, and decisive to be effective. For President Trump, some would say his toolbox is limited, but to others, he is bringing all of his business skills to bear even if he uses them as a hammer.

I'LL TELL YOU WHEN WE GET THERE

- *A written vision and plan still matters; people like to see a roadmap.*

A vision matters. A plan matters. Not the nonsense vision that claims to build the world's best flux capacitor with gold framistams by the end of the new millennium. The plan needs to be credible and at the same time be inspirational. Great leaders announce visions and plans, and the believers will run through walls to bring the plan to fruition. Vision and planning are areas where many leaders fall short because of lack of clarity. We need to know where we are going and how we will get there. Even if it is only directionally correct, the vision and the plan are required. The "Make America Great Again" vision needs a little more meat on those bones.

SOMETIMES YOU JUST NEED TO START SOMEWHERE

- *Complex problems rarely have simple solutions.*

Immigration policy revision is complex. Trade policy with the European Union is like a tangled knot. Military actions and plans are multifaceted. Building a Space Force for the next century is mind-boggling. Unraveling trade agreements is a headache waiting to happen. What to do? Just start. The act of beginning will at least move thinking and resources in that direction. And starting sends the message that things might change, that something is getting done. Trump is good at starting. What the finish looks like is TBD.

RUNNING THROUGH THE BUSHES AND BRAMBLES

- *People will figure out their own organization chart if one does not exist.*

"Who is my boss?" is a pretty simple question but sometimes it is more difficult to answer than it needs to be. When the org chart is full of people with the title of Interim, anything does that mean someone is on probation or that he or she is only a placeholder until we find someone else. The Trump administration makes no apologies for all the open positions at senior levels in the government. In spite of all of the open positions, the government keeps operating. People are making it work because of their commitment to their careers. Maybe some jobs don't need to be filled again. Maybe the wheels will fall off the bus. Hmmmm. Leaving important positions is a risk that Trump is willing to take. He claims, "His whole life is a bet" and he is taking on in this regard.

DID THE ISRAELI EMBASSY MOVE?

- *People only care about what directly affects them.*

People care about anything and everything that a President does, but those same people care about some things more than others. Opioids, drug prices, MS-13 gangs, tax cuts, and federal regulations affect lots of people so lots of people care about those topics. Donald Trump knows this leadership bromide and spends time on the things people care about. It may be at the expense of other issues that he should spend time on like foreign policy and filling open cabinet positions, but by gum, he knows where to spend his leadership capital.

GOING TO HELL BUT SURE ENJOYING THE RIDE

- *How long do you stick with something you know will not work?*

The leader's commitment to the plan is important to success. If the leader isn't committed, why should anyone else care? The leader needs to be willing to abandon initiatives that are not working even though there is an implied admission of making a mistake, something Donald Trump is not willing to ever admit. The cost of continuing something that everyone knows will not work is too expensive in leadership capital and for the organization. If it's not working, give it up and move on. People will appreciate the relief.

WHERE THE RUBBER MEETS THE SKY

- *There is no honeymoon period for leaders.*

The day after his inauguration, Donald Trump was criticized for overestimating the size of the crowd at his inauguration ceremony. Well that didn't take long for his grace period as a new leader to be over. Leaders face the "what have you done for me lately" problem of short memories and short-term perspectives. Results matter even in small increments. Presidential decrees or orders can get the ball rolling on implementation, even in the short term. Trump moved quickly to initiate executive orders and attempted to live up to campaign promises. Some worked.

WITCH HUNTS AND IMPEACHMENTS ARE ANNOYING

- *When in survival mode, it's hard to do your job.*

A leader can never accomplish his or her agenda when on trial. All those witnesses and testimony can be a big distraction. Whether an impeachment or fighting to keep the job, the leader has two choices. One is to ignore the entire process as best one can and continue to do the business at hand. If this is the choice, you can continue to point to progress. The other option is to go all in and disparage witnesses and call all attacks a hoax and a big waste of time. In the meantime, nothing much gets done. Like Donald Trump, it's hard not to go for the second choice and defend oneself. It's a bet.

3

Communications — Can It Be Too Much?

Check out any employee survey in any organization and the number one issue that will come up is communications. As in, "I don't know what's going on…" so how am I supposed to contribute or support a leader. It's a universal problem. But ask most leaders and he or she will claim that communications is all they seem to do. The problem is compounded by new technologies that make communications easier but more fraught with nuance and interpretation. Donald Trump is big on communications, no matter the message.

WHY BEAT AROUND THE BUSH...?

- *Tweets as a communication tool can send an emotion as well as a message. High drama can be delivered in all caps or bold fonts.*

Tweets can be your best friend and worst enemy. BDT (Before Donald Trump), Twitter was not an accepted communication tool for leaders. Now it is and it has proven to be both effective and efficient. Other leaders are now using it to communicate quickly to complex and far-flung recipients. Not only that, he can communicate his irritation, frustration, or pleasure through the tweet in a direct manner. We are never going back to the internal corporate newsletter. Why have an all-hands meeting when you can tweet to the world? In every organization, when it comes to issues, communications will always be the number one issue. Tweets don't solve it.

CAN YOU HEAR ME NOW?

- *Everything you say is on the record and can impact strategy, perceptions, and execution effectiveness. Off-handed comments can come back to haunt you.*

Off-handed comments for leaders are not off hand. Casual comments spoken in the hallway are not casual when a leader makes them. Off-color jokes will offend someone. Racist jokes or comments will get you fired – usually. (And should.) Once said, any comment is out there and attempts at revisionist explanations will fall flat. Assume the cameras are always rolling and assume they were rolling in the past and that what you say will be compared to what you said then. Anything you say can come back to haunt you, even years later. May as well own up to the comment, own it, or apologize. Or, as Mr. Trump is likely to do, it happened, ignore it, just move on.

IT WAS IN THE MIDDLE OF A BAD DAY...

- *Think before you tweet. A bad tweet can be like drunk dialing and get you in trouble from which you will never recover. And they linger. Even if your tweets are voluminous, the weird ones will be gleaned.*

Excuses won't get you far. There it is. The tweet is out, and they are hard to take back. It may have been an emotional outburst or maybe you really were drunk, the send, post, or share button is not your friend. The F-bomb is front and center and maybe comments about sex organs or calling people's spouses' names. No matter. Tweeting is not different than sending an email or leaving a message that you regret. A bad tweet can bring unwanted attention, get you fired, or worse. Sometimes the President needs to think before he tweets.

I NEVER SAID THAT!...

- *Keep your antennae up for times that you are being recorded.*

Although you should always be aware, sometimes you just don't know when you are being recorded. If your voice is on the tape, it can be difficult to dismiss. The defense can be the comments were taken out of context or it was only a joke. Or, as in Donald Trump's case, you can deny any statement with a wink and the knowledge that many of your supporters were secretly thinking the same thing. The result will be the supporters claiming again and again that "he says what I am thinking".

LET ME CLARIFY WHAT I MEANT

- *A taped interview or phone call can be helpful when motives are questioned. Or not.*

Even though the words were said, and even though they were caught on tape, maybe the words didn't mean what they sounded like. Maybe they were taken out of context. Maybe the tape that recorded them was faulty. Maybe the person who taped the words is untrustworthy. In all cases, clarifying what was meant vs. what was said can be useful for a leader. Or, in spite of the facts, ignore the whole thing as Mr. Trump is wont to do.

THE BROKEN RECORD STRATEGY...

- *Repeating things, even if not true, might get you to begin to believe them. The more you repeat, the more you believe. Others may or may not follow. Repeating something that everyone knows is not true will not make it true no matter how many times you say it.*

We've all done it, repeated stories that get a little better all the time. Our high school heroics get better; our resumes are slightly enhanced; our travels are expanded, and after repeating the tales so many times, they become fact in our own mind. That doesn't make them true. All the more important for a leader is to not repeat embellished stories about crowd size or accomplishments. People know the truth even if you forget it. Accurate and clear key messages are the stock and trade of leaders. It's better if the key messages are true. Repeating something that is not true just digs a deeper hole every time. Surrounding yourself with people who will tell you the truth is a good group to have around.

WHEN EMPHASIS IS REQUIRED!

- *To any statement, you can always add the following for emphasis: Believe Me!*

Exclamation points are a new aspect to leadership. Donald Trump uses them each day as if to emphasize the point and ensure that people know that he means it. He adds the phrase "Believe Me" for emphasis as well. Maybe it's a New York thing. Maybe it's the style of a salesman/deal maker. Maybe it's the way to create a headline that we want to be the lead story tomorrow. It is part of his brand but is unusual for a leader. The exclamation points and the all caps and the emphasis don't make any comments more credible, but all the commotion makes them more prominent and shapes a story.

BEFORE YOU HIT THE SEND BUTTON...

- *Timing of tweet is just as important as the message.*

Sometimes the importance of a tweet varies based on the time it was sent. A 2:00 am tweet might be seen as drunken message and unfortunate but forgiven. A tweet about someone who is testifying before congress while he or she is actually testifying is a sign that the tweet sender is worried. Leaders need to know when to get involved and when to lay off and let events take a natural course. As the President knows and uses to his advantage, a tweet can disrupt a trial, a hearing, a football game, or the stock market. A tweet can be a weapon.

GOOD QUESTION, LET ME ANSWER A DIFFERENT ONE

- *Shifting the narrative is a storyteller's skill.*

When the economy is booming, don't talk about good times with adult entertainers. When the unemployment rate is at a historic low, don't talk about tax returns. Controlling the narrative is the silver bullet for leaders to shape perceptions about performance. To lose that control is to have others paint a picture of you that may or may not be accurate or what is going to help you keep your job. Sending tweets of disruption, bold statements, or crazy talk is a way to control that narrative. Or, having impromptu press conferences with the sound of helicopters whirring in the background is a way to deliver bold messages too.

THE TRUMP SECRET CODE

- *People examine a tweet for hidden messages including what time it was sent, punctuation, capital letters, and dangling modifiers.*

Maybe a tweet is just a tweet. Or maybe there is more? Are there hidden meanings in the white space of tweets? Is Twitter part of the diabolical cunning of management? Does the reference to a nuclear bomb mean a war might be happening? If a name is misspelled does it mean that person is about to be fired? Stop trying to read the tweet leaves; it's a waste of emotional currency. A tweet is a tweet until, collectively, they make for a crazy leader who spends his or her time on Twitter.

MEET ME IN MONTANA

- *Talking only to supporters will confirm your message but won't win over any new supporters.*

Given the choice, would you rather talk to people who like you or people who would speed up to hit you in the parking lot? It is not as much fun to talk to people who disagree with your decisions and behavior. Like current thinking of building on one's strengths rather than trying to improve on weaknesses; building the supporter base rather than converting detractors could make sense. The numbers of supporters or detractors may dictate which way to go. Sometimes you must convert the naysayers in order to be successful.

PLEASE KEEP IT IN THIS ROOM

- *There are no secrets in any organization.*

No matter how many "I will not ever tell" one hears, the confidential information will get out. No matter how many confidentiality documents are signed or Bibles sworn upon, information will be spread. As it spreads, the level of accuracy will diminish. Remember the game "playing telephone". Donald Trump understands this so he avoids the charade and just blurts out what should probably be kept secret. It may not be the safest way to share state secrets but it is efficient.

THE WEEK-AT-A-GLANCE BOOK DOESN'T LIE

- *A leader's calendar is the barometer of what's important.*

The options of where to go, who to meet with can be mind-boggling. Internal or external? Constituents or staff? Boy scouts or foreign leaders? The truth is borne out in any leader's calendar. For a President, the calendar is a matter of public record. Notations that are less than transparent such as "planning time" or "private time" will be eyed suspiciously. Time off or golf time will be eyed as slacking off although everyone agrees that a job such as President requires downtime. Creating the balance is what is important. Donald Trump seems to play a lot of golf at his own resorts.

I WANNA TALK ABOUT ME

- *It is not always about you. It is probably not about you. Don't make it about you. If it is about you, it is probably not good. More likely, "it" is about solving problems and moving forward.*

The research is in. Weak leaders hoard power. Strong leaders share power. All the books say so. Sometimes it feels like without you there would be no problems solved or the world would swirl down the toilet. Think about the most successful organizations and you will probably think about the team, not one person. Making any success about only you will mean also that any failure is about …YOU.

WHAT IS COVFEFE?

- *An effective spokesperson can make a leader's life better and buffer the heat of criticism. As long as they too tell the truth.*

Maybe the most important person on the senior team is the spokesperson, front person, PR person, communications director, or mouthpiece. Call the role what you will, the spokesperson is on the battle line trying to explain things, good or bad. The more changes that a leader plans to make, the more important the spokesperson is to fight off attacks and make it easier to understand the rationale for any change. In some cases, the spokesperson may have to explain made-up words or tweets of rage with mixed results. If the cast of Saturday Night Live makes fun of your spokesperson, something may be not quite right.

I DON'T KNOW, BUT THAT IS WHAT PEOPLE ARE TELLING ME...

- *Confusing others, dilution of the facts, or wild caveats can be a communications strategy. It doesn't last long.*

"Hundreds of people have told me this" is a comment that will lead to the follow-up question: "Who are those hundreds of people? What are their names?" Facts are an important tool for a leader, especially if what you say is in defense of something you are doing. Just like, "sarcasm is the truth masked in humor", an allusion to what people are telling you means you believe what people are telling you. **Better to say what you think instead of what unknown people are telling you.**

SHAKEN, NOT STIRRED...

- *In critical situations, stay on script. Deliver the message without side comments or emotions. The more important the situation, the more important to stay on message. Think Abraham Lincoln at Gettysburg.*

Nuance is not necessarily your friend. Nuance can change the message. Nuance can say, "This wasn't my decision"; or, "My staff is making me do this"; or, "If it was up to me, I wouldn't be saying this..." And in so doing, the message is lost because the nuanced message is delivered over the content. It's like when a parent makes a child apologize but all involved know it is a forced "I'm sorry". Nuance can include rolling of the eyes, smiles, smirks, side-eye glances, furrowed brows, or just plain unhappy faces. Body language can be more important than what is said.

4

Hiring and Firing Is a Blood Sport

"It wouldn't be difficult to be a leader if it wasn't for people". I have heard that statement more than once as leaders grapple with people issues. And there are always people issues. Dealing with people quickly is a strength for a leader. No leader I know ever said, "I fired that person way too soon". Donald Trump may be the exception as he hires and fires people faster than we can keep track. Some experts believe the fastest way to create organizational change is to fire everyone. If Trump wants to create organizational change, maybe he is on the right track.

AVAILABILITY IS NOT A SKILL

- *Bringing children into the business is a saw that cuts many ways. Think twice before the "special assistant" role is filled with a son or daughter or any in-laws.*

Maybe Johnnie or Sarah can't find a job after that high-priced college education. Maybe they are not sure what exactly they want to do...Law school? Travel? Save the world? How about get into the family enterprise!? Such a proposition presents an opportunity for learning and development and a chance to move them out of the house and into the office. But, if ill prepared, a big assignment could mean disaster and problems within the family. Depending on the position and the responsibilities, the family is often thrown into the deep water without any floaties. Negotiating peace agreements and diplomatic breakthroughs requires skills not learned around the kitchen table. Don't set family members up to fail. The world is littered with movies and real life where the kids were put into a spot "to learn" with disastrous results. There are exceptions.

ONE BAD APPLE...

- *A rogue team member can hurt effectiveness and create distractions to the entire organization. Especially if they write books.*

There **are** times when a leader's instincts come into play and team members who go sideways should not be a surprise to an effective leader. The behavior could be passive aggressive or just plain aggressive. The behavior could mean ignoring the goals and going off on a rogue mission. The behavior could mean, "I am looking for another job, but I will stay here until I find it." Change out team members before the rogue behavior happens. No one ever acted on a rogue team member too soon. The tell-all book will be released in any case.

TAKE THIS JOB AND SHOVE IT...

- *Constantly living under the ax of being fired (most of the Trump team) does not improve performance. It's like tailgating – it doesn't make the person in front of you go faster.*

A wise teamster once told me, "If you are worried about your job, you probably should be". He went on to say with teamster wisdom, "If you are constantly threatened about losing your job, your 'give-a-shit factor' goes way down". Publicly criticizing others will make them worry and probably care less but hate you. Hanging others out to dry will hurt performance, and lack of support will make you look bad and create sympathy for others. Good leaders don't want people around them to cower for fear of losing their jobs. It's just another form of bullying by bombastic leaders.

THE WHEELS WILL FALL OFF THE BUS

- *Maybe those unfilled and desperate required roles that need to be filled really don't need to be filled.*

Wheels rarely fall off buses and so it is true when seemingly important jobs go unfilled. Although on any given day there could be hundreds or thousands of unfilled jobs in the Trump administration, most would say that in spite of those openings, their life hasn't changed much. In fact, the sense is that we may be saving tax dollars that can be redistributed to more important issues. The vacancies might result in longer-term issues, but in the meantime, we are learning that wheels on the bus go round and round regardless of the number of unfilled jobs.

WHO IS YOUR BOSS?

- *I can get you fired and I am not afraid to do that…*

Chains of command matter, it's not just in the military. The lines on an organization chart matter. People want to know the lines of authority and who is ultimately making decisions. Chaos ensues when leaders disrupt those chains and lines. Why bother doing analysis or making recommendations if someone at the top is going to swoop in and make all the decisions based on instinct anyway. Shadow foreign policy or parallel structures create confusion and the best outcome may be elusive. Others who are credible may testify to that effect as has been seen.

IT TAKES ALL KINDS OF KINDS

- *The "best people" is a relative term.*

The best people may not be your friends or the ones who are all alike or the ones who happen to be available. The best people are the ones who have the best skills and attributes for the job at hand. Best people means also that they complement each other and build on each other's strengths. The best people means the leader looks high and low for talent and includes those not usually considered, usually called diversity. The "best people" should be held in awe by others based on their background, skills, and enthusiasm for the job.

I'M NOT THE ONLY ONE

- *What might get others fired doesn't mean you will be fired for the same offense. Or, you can be fired for an offense that others commit and they get to keep their jobs. Make sense?*

Make a list of all the things that could get you fired. You know the list, include telling a racist joke; using your position for financial gain; cheating on expense accounts; sexual harassment; lying to legal authorities; or, anything that happens at the annual sales meeting after midnight. The list that applies to you is the one that requires attention. Some leaders can retain their jobs while committing unthinkable offenses to our sense of what is right. Others will get canned for minor offenses. Leaders should act like they are in the second category. In most jobs, Donald Trump would have been fired by now.

DODGEBALL IS NOT A FUN SPORT

- *Dodging insults results in a lot of activity but not much in the way of results.*

Colleagues should not duck and cover at the sight of a leader. Leaders should not be so impetuous and impulsive that others hide. Leaders should be the same person every day and we all hope that person is the one we need to hide from. Leaders should not be accused of having multiple personalities. A President who is constantly throwing barbs and insults is destined to get a bunch back. It's like email – if you send a lot of emails, you will receive a bunch back. Don't complain.

LAST ONE OUT, TURN OUT THE LIGHTS

- *Turnover is not a problem; it is a symptom of a problem. People need reasons to leave a job; it is not a random occurrence.*

When people are racing for the door, the high rate of turnover is cited as a huge problem. But why are the people racing for the door? It's because they are dealing with a job they don't like. It could be because of an asshole boss or low pay or high stress or any number of issues. Worse, turnover is contagious. The way to stop turnover is change. Change behavior, change the environment, change leaders. Turnover requires the change of something or maybe everything.

THE HATCHET MAN COMETH...

- *Being known for firing people is not the brand you want. Sometimes people do need to be fired but don't build your management style on it.*

It is no fun to be fired. It should be no fun to fire others. At least in my experience it is no fun. Sometimes people deserve to be fired; nonetheless, there is no joy in the execution. It can be the ultimate power play. Make any termination fast and sensitive but not an activity for pride. The executioner is never welcome in the village. President Trump has built a tough guy reputation on his willingness to pull the trigger fast and say, "You're Fired!" He may be the only one ever who could build that brand and then get elected in a popular election.

TEST DRIVES ARE FREE

- *Fill open positions with "Acting" people.*

Any leader is being evaluated every day. Anyone in an acting role is not only evaluated every day but is on a sort of probation. Is the "acting" person filling the role until someone better can be found or are we all just waiting for a final approval? In either case, it's a tough position for the acting person but a good position for the leader. If it doesn't work out, the acting period just ends and the person goes away. If it does work out, the leader is brilliant in converting the acting person to an official capacity. Creating acting positions also raises the questions, Why was the position even created? Do we need that position?

TAKE THE HILL, PLEASE

- *Surrounding yourself with people with military backgrounds can be helpful at creating discipline and a plan. Aggression can be checked at the door.*

Life for a leader is a continuum of creating plans, executing on those plans, and special projects. Neither MBA training or instructional YouTube videos can match the experience that a military background can bring to bear on plans and project management. However, when everyone around the table is wearing a military uniform, the perspectives may be skewed. Not every problem requires a military solution or assessment. Having nonmilitary perspectives will bring diversity as well. For a leader, sometimes it's all about diversity.

5

About the Critics – Can They All Be Wrong?

A leader who doesn't attract critics is probably a leader who is not taking bold enough actions. Sometimes there are a lot of critics. And anonymous critics have nothing to lose so they can rant and scream without ever fearing for their own reputation. Critics can be a leader's worst nightmare but can also keep a crazy leader in check and redirect actions. Obsessing over critics will make any leader impotent in doing the job.

IF YOU DON'T LIKE MY TWANG

- *Critics are sometimes correct, sometimes not. Critics are not always wrong. Just because they are after you, doesn't mean they shouldn't be.*

Critics can be tough and focus on all the things you don't want to hear. How many performance reviews start out with the sentence "You know you are doing really well so let me focus on the areas that need drastic improvement". We like feedback, so long as it is full of superlatives. We don't like the critical kind. But the voice of critics might ring true even though we may not like to admit it. Before dismissing the critics, if the chorus is all singing the same critical song, it is time to listen and think of options.

I LOOKED UNDER THE COVERS…

- *Independent investigations will always find something, big or small.*

Dread is the only word that comes to mind when an independent investigator is retained for any matters related to leadership activities. Did I put too many miles on my expense report? Is there a photo with my hand clasping that gin and tonic? If you did, the investigators will find out.

BUT IT JUST MAY BE A LUNATIC YOU'RE LOOKING FOR...

- *When you are called "unfit" for your job, it's time to pay attention.*

The word "unfit" is a pretty harsh indictment. When used, the word could imply physical limitations or credentials but it gets worse. The word "unfit" is usually going after mental or emotional qualifications that are lacking. In other words, an unfit leader is unbalanced, unhinged, or just plain psychotic. Leaders should not be in any of these categories. When called unfit, the time is nigh to see someone to ascertain the provenance and worry.

WHEN EVERYONE IS ABOVE AVERAGE

- *Performance reviews for leaders happen every day.*

No one likes performance reviews whether you are a leader or in the bowels of the organization. For a leader, there is no six-month cycle, performance reviews happen every day. Every day. Whether it be through employee surveys, comments on Twitter, or polls, a leader receives feedback whether it is desired or not. Some leaders will change based on the feedback, others ignore it. Some feedback may be about hairstyles or golf scores; other feedback may be about international treaties or nuclear weapon policy. Most feedback merits attention, but it is more important to know which is important and which is not. Of course, it is always true that all feedback can be ignored, and making decisions and implementing them without disregard to feedback can save a lot of time.

BAD SITUATIONS CAN ALWAYS TURN WORSE

- *Always think, "What is the worst that can happen to me?"*

It's usually not so bad. However, if the term orange jumpsuits are included in the answer, it's best to consider other alternatives. The situation can turn worse when there is deceit or fraud along the way that will almost always be unearthed. For any leader, coming forward and explaining the bad situation and taking any responsibility for what happened is the best thing to do. Ask Richard Nixon and lots of other leaders about the merits of cover-ups.

GET THEM BEFORE THEY GET YOU

- *Always be on offense.*

Always operating on offense doesn't mean one needs to be offensive. It means wake up early and put the rest of the world on defense before they even wake up. Offense could mean creating a crisis, getting everyone's attention, and solving the crisis (or not) before you move on. The news cycle is waiting for this to happen and will respond each day accordingly. Being on the offensive every day will not allow anyone to recover, especially the press, and in the confusion, there is credit to be taken and accomplishments to boast about.

UH, OH

- *Surprises are almost never about something good about to happen*

Surprises come in many forms, but leaders in general don't like them. If the surprise is a good one, it is always welcome. If the surprise is bad, someone will get blamed or fired. The faux pas will definitely go on the permanent record. But leaders too have a responsibility not to surprise as well. Surprise decisions are often knee-jerk reactions that are just as often difficult to recover from. Donald Trump is a leader full of surprises.

BEWARE OF THE CIRCULAR FIRING SQUAD

- *When everyone is shooting at each other, someone will get shot.*

The Trump administration is noted for turnover. Each time someone leaves the administration, he or she runs across the street to a literary agent to sign a book deal. In the new book, the criticism of the President and his team comes out. The book might be a best-seller until the next book criticizing the President and his team comes out. Each time, the perception of the President and his team is reinforced and there is not much new to learn. A team that is always a criticizing each other is not a high-performing team.

It's a good thing the President is not much of a reader.

A BULLETPROOF VEST CAN BE A FASHION ACCESSORY

- *PTSD can happen to leaders too.*

Leadership almost always involves stress. It's the decision-making that's required causes the stress and anxiety. As in, the constant self-questioning, "Am I doing the right thing?" Sometimes leaders have to choose among several options that can change people's lives. Sometimes a leader chooses among limited options, none of which are good. Just think of the pressure that any President is under with decisions often involving life or death situations. It never ends, and some Presidents deal with it better than others. Leaders like Donald Trump are able to compartmentalize their issues and life in general. The ability to do that will cut down on that PTSD tendency.

HOW CAN THEY BE SURE?

- *Questioning intelligence agencies and spies is a risky business.*

It's a brave leader who questions the intelligence community. The phrase "If I tell you I will have to kill you" was not created without some real-life reference. People who risk their lives to be patriotic and serve the public greater good are usually not prone to act at odds to their organization or country. Probably, there are exceptions, but a leader who turns the intelligence crowd is a leader who might have a separate security detail. And while the leader is at it, don't make the military mad at you. They are on the same team as you.

THEY CAN'T ALL BE WRONG. OR CAN THEY?

- *When all advisors abandon you, it might be time to reconsider some ideas.*

Watch for signals. Smart people can have differing opinions but not all of the smart people. If there is a sense that only those who are not paying attention are the ones who are in your camp, it may be time to take stock. The Business Roundtable that President Trump put together was comprised of CEOs, most would contend pretty smart people. They all quit. None are left to advise the President. Some would say they are a bunch of prima donnas and he doesn't need them. Others might ask, "Can they all be wrong?" Donald Trump asked for the help of the Roundtable, they all quit, and he is not worried about the advice he is not receiving. Outside counsellors are always helpful.

ONLY THE PARANOID SURVIVE

- *Sometimes others really are after you.*

Paranoia can be healthy for a leader because others probably ARE after you. A leader thinks that way. Andy Grove, former CEO at Intel, coined the paranoia phrase while he was riding on top of one of the most successful companies in the world. Paranoia in this sense doesn't mean constant suspicion and agitation. It does mean being aware of those who are competing with you and those who can help you. No diagnosis is implied but paranoia is a strength that Mr. Trump manipulates to change staffing and policy. It may not be a bad characteristic in manageable doses.

AND NEVER, EVER READ THE COMMENTS

- *The higher the level achieved, the thicker the skin required.*

Donald Trump was booed at a World Series baseball game. He was cheered at a football game in Alabama. He should not have been surprised in either case; to say he is a polarizing President is an understatement. Leaders need to bask in the support of the most ardent supporters and build armor to protect themselves from the critics. One hopes there will always be those supporters. Hurt feelings are not part of leadership, but they are part of human nature. Like Donald Trump, leaders need to spend time and energy with those who will show you love and be prepared for those who shoot barbs.

6

Is Loyalty Just a Four-Letter Word?

We wrestle with loyalty. We want to be loyal to something. To whom and what can we be loyal? What cause or mission deserves our loyalty? These are big questions that deserve bit answers. Loyalty is a precious commodity and should not be toyed with. We are loyal to our families, our alma maters, and our dogs are loyal to us. Do leaders deserve our loyalty? Yes, but it has to be earned.

YOU HAVE THE RIGHT TO REMAIN SILENT...

- *Your biggest supporters will turn on you if it is in their own best interest. Every time.*

People love you until they don't. "I would take a bullet for him" is only true until the bullet is on the way. It doesn't have to be the threat of an orange jumpsuit that will make supporters turn although that is a guarantee that people will turn on you. It could be disagreement about strategy, promotion disappointments, or the elimination of free coffee. It could be that supporters are just tired of listening to you boast or fib. Big numbers of supporters can dwindle quickly based on actions that may not seem significant but peck away at loyalty. Donald Trump has learned who is steadfast in their loyalty and who is not. The question often, to whom or what is Trump loyal?

NOW IS MY CHANCE...

- *Anonymous sources on performance can be dangerous and often believed. Feedback systems that allow for anonymity will be mean.*

Feedback systems are a good source of information. When you hear from trusted advisors about how you are doing, it is a time to listen. Those who care about the organization's success are never anonymous and will always provide feedback that is best for the organization. When you hear from anonymous sources the venom can come out. Ask anyone who is active on social media about anonymity. Ask anyone who has gone through a 360-degree review about anonymity. Anonymous sources are sometimes right, but they are often vindictive and a channel to get even. The real problem is that those anonymous sources are often believed when the book comes out. And there are lots of books. Be wary.

ACT LIKE YOU LOVE ME

- *Spousal relationships send out signals to others as to what kind of leader/person you are. Others will closely watch what kind of relationship you have with your spouse and will make judgments.*

It shouldn't matter, but it does. How you and your spouse treat each other sends out signals and can impact your role in the organization. If you beat each other up, your time in professional sports or as a college administrator is limited. If you and your spouse live in two different cities, others might suspect that all is not well at home and you are distracted. If revelations about past affairs are making headlines, it means things can't be good at home. The cold shoulder or the brush-off seen on camera is a sign that you are spending time trying to work on a relationship instead of doing your job. Time for a change? Spousal support makes for a happier career so make sure your spouse approves of career decisions.

───────────

WILL YOUR LAWYER TALK TO GOD FOR YOU?

- *Lawyers can be your friends or not.*

No lawyer jokes are required in order to pick on the legal profession. Love'em or hate'em, if you are a leader, lawyers are a part of your life. Lawyers should both interpret the law and provide counsel on tricky matters. They are called counselors for a reason and that is how they should be used. A leader who dispatches a personal lawyer to do official business may be playing with potential conflicts and confusion. An effective leader knows how to use official and personal lawyers to be effective. Those two types of lawyers should not be in conflict. The more lawyers a leader has around, the more controversial the leader and his or her actions. Donald Trump is a good example.

WHAT WERE ONCE MEMORIES
ARE NOW EVIDENCE

- *Even if you apologize or pay off people for past sins, the people and the sins come back to haunt you.*

The world now has a very long memory. What was written in high school yearbooks is now subject to review. In fact, for a leader, any and all actions, past and present, are open to review and inspection by nearly anyone who has access to a computer, which is everyone. Even more important, the actions of the past are seen through the lenses of today. What was "horseplay" in 1960 is assault today. It's too late to retract what was written in those old yearbooks, but it's not too late to reform and refrain from any new boorish or worse behavior. Donald Trump has changed the standard on past behaviors but there are still standards. Pay attention.

LET IT GO, LET IT FLOW

- *A team that works together will get things done. A team that is quarreling and stabbing each other in the back will try to make it through the day until they can find another job.*

At one time or another, we have all been in that special place. It could have been a team or a club or a job and it was a special thing and you even knew it at the time. The group felt like it was getting great things done together and the rest of the world couldn't compare. During the course of a career, it doesn't happen often, but after it happens once, you want it to happen again. It was a time and place where people who liked each other were able to get extraordinary things done. Most of us have also been on the other side of that special place – the place where happiness and productivity go to die. In that case, sometimes the only solution is to let the entire team go and start all over. The Trump administration has spun through several turnovers for better or worse.

THE WINGMAN COMETH

- *A second-in-command who never ever strays from your script can make life easier.*

Every Batman has a Robin. Every *Don Quixote* has a Sancho Panza. Every leader needs that special person who is loyal, helpful, and trustworthy. That person is a rarity and should be appreciated. He or she can be in charge while the leader is on vacation and can defend policies and programs that may not make sense. The second-in-command may not be likable, dynamic, or ready to be in charge, but while they are acting as number two, there is never any revolt or second-guessing. The number two is, above all else, LOYAL. Every leader needs a go-to-number-two.

I AM GOING TO COUNT TO THREE...

- *Empty threats are empty.*

Who hasn't seen a parent threaten a child with empty threats? "One, no one pays attention, Two, maybe I will consider change, Three!" And the child shrugs. Even a child sees right through empty threats and goes ahead with whatever mischief they might have been in. The same holds true for empty threats from leaders. Once a threat is seen as empty, the leader's credibility is suspect. And when it comes to hints of an invasion or an attack, others will hope the threat is empty but it causes trauma and drama all around. Making no threats unless really required is the best strategy. If threats are made, if others believe the leader will follow through to the threat, it can bring real stature to the leader. Threats with adjectives and exclamation points, like Trump issues, can be effective because no one is sure if they are real or empty threats.

I SMELL A RAT

- *Direct reports who conspire against you should be confronted and dealt with quickly.*

Loyalty among colleagues cannot be overrated. A direct report who is disloyal will hurt any leader, sometimes in subtle ways. Think "one bad apple" and all that. Disloyalty can mean being an anonymous source to the press, it could mean a lack of respect, it could mean constant second-guessing, it could mean not implementing a plan, or it could mean just inactivity with passive aggressive flavors. Firing anyone who is not loyal is a way to engender loyalty.

7

Being Current and Doing Homework

The scouts might be right, being prepared is the secret to survival for a leader. Playing catch-up every day is a stressful way to operate and not very effective. Being prepared is a function of listening to smart people, reading what is important, and understanding what has gone before. It's not complicated, it just takes time and an attention span. Most importantly, it takes a willingness to learn.

MEASURE TWICE, CUT ONCE...

- *Preparedness is a virtue. Never underestimate the power of being prepared. The more difficult the problem, issue, or decision, the more important it is to be well prepared.*

Some things really are important, read the backup materials, read the manuals. Listen to people who know what they are talking about. Do the analysis and look at what has been done before. Put the "D" in Diligence. We all know the difference between being prepared and not. Prepared is better. Stress is less and results are better. "Winging it" or following instincts will get you as far as "I wish I was better prepared". Lack of preparedness is the reason we still have nightmares about showing up at school in our underwear and being surprised by an exam. "I don't need to prepare" are famous last words.

WHEN YOU STOP LEARNING, YOU DIE

- *Reinventing yourself can make many turns. Business to entertainment to something else is a journey to embrace.*

Reinvention can mean moving from a real estate mogul to a world leader. Or, it can mean moving from a carpenter to a poet or any of the millions of options that are presented. All the research on aging indicates that the way to stay healthy is to stay vibrant and to continue to learn. Reinvention can be invigorating and scary, but it presents the thrill of change and the trying something new. When reinventing yourself, don't get into a spot where you are over your head.

COMES FROM A LONG LINE

- *Understand the history of the role you play in the organization.*

Unless it's a start-up or a brand-new organization, there are always precedents and protocols that are established. Whether or not to pay attention to the precedents is one of the leader's first decisions. Some traditions are sacred and should always be kept while others are best thrown into the green bin. The bigger the job and the longer the job has been around means, there are more decisions to be made about what traditions to keep or what ones to start. Any CEO ever at Apple will have to recognize the traditions that Steve Jobs started. Any President of Harvard will have to recognize the traditions there and choose what is important today. The key is to discern what traditions are so important that they cannot be toyed with, like the State of the Union Address. Others can go, and good riddance.

THERE'S YOUR TROUBLE

- *Spending time to understand issues is time well spent.*

Call it homework or preparation or anything you want that implies to you, the leader is ready. Homework doesn't need to be calculus or organic chemistry, there are others who do that. A leader needs to know where he or she is all the time. It may sound overly basic but knowing the location, what is happening in that location, who the people are in that location will position the leader as someone who is current and aware and can provide hope that things will get better, no matter how good or bad they are. For a leader to not know the location and what is important to those in that position will send out a message of being clueless or not caring. For a busy leader, as President Trump knows, it can be confusing without a summary briefing.

WHERE IS THAT REMOTE?

- *Getting all information from one source may not give you the data you need to make decisions.*

We know leaders watch television, who doesn't binge on *Breaking Bad?* But we don't want to know that much about any leader's TV habits. We don't want leaders to develop policies or programs based on what was just seen on Fox TV or CNN. In fact, one hopes that leaders have better things to do than watch TV. TV, or now Twitter, can be the best way to get a message to a leader once the screen habits are known. TV can be an escape and a communications tool, it should not be the major source of information for any leader.

TOGA! TOGA! TOGA!

- *It is possible to skate through college but…*

Eventually you will wish you paid more attention in statistics or history or economics. The toga parties are fun but few leadership positions have the luxury of getting by on social skills. Leadership means gathering data, listening to others, examining the options and then, finally, making a decision. That can't happen through slacking off on the details. Pattern recognition can also play into any knowledge base. If you've seen it before, you know what might be required. Collecting data does have an ending but "analysis paralysis" is not a malady Donald Trump will ever be accused of.

IT'S HARD TO KEEP UP

- *Read, be current. Know the latest. Read The NY Times from cover to cover.*

On any given day there could be scientific breakthroughs, regional conflicts, important film launched, major sport championships, mass shootings, and a litany of other events that disrupt the world and could have an impact on an organization. Like the old song says, "the shin bone connected to the thigh bone...", everything is connected and understanding those interrelationships is an important part of decision-making. It is understandable that no one can know everything but it is not ok for a leader to revel in a lack of worldly understanding. An effective leader will surround the room with others who, collectively, should know everything. Even if the press is your enemy, as Donald Trump thinks, you still need to read what they are writing.

BASED ON A TRUE STORY

- *Keeping records is good for memoirs and remembering what happened day to day.*

Note-taking which includes the time, date, and what was discussed in any meeting or phone call is a skill that most junior analysts learn to develop. Look for all those Moleskine notebooks in the backpacks. When called later to make a presentation or recite what happened, those notes cannot be more valuable. The same holds true when called to testify before congress. The more accurate the notes, the more they can stand up to attack. Foreign Service Officers learn this skill too. As the leader, it is sometimes difficult to take notes but at least try to jot things down later. Being right doesn't mean everyone else is wrong. Neither does being critical of others mean they are wrong.

HAPPY DAYS ARE HERE AGAIN

- *A roaring economy is a time for big ideas.*

When people have good jobs and enjoy regular paychecks, they tend to like the leader no matter who it is. In a company that's growing and giving out bonuses, the employees love the leader and will allow for lots of foibles. A President who presides over a booming economy will or at least should be popular. Any President who served during a recession or down economy learned that lesson. If "it's the economy, stupid", then the focus should be to keep the economy booming and front and center. Building on healthy results is an opportunity to do more and set up the future. Donald Trump is a leader who has the power to move markets and effect lives like few others. It is a power that should not be taken lightly.

RUNS GREAT, NEEDS ENGINE

- *Details are more important than superlatives.*

"Really great" is a good way to describe how you are feeling on any given day. "Beautiful" is a way to describe a bright sunny morning. Some will take issue if a phone call between two heads of state in which millions of dollars of military help is described as beautiful. Leaders need to understand what is going on around them which almost always means understanding some of the details involved in any situation. Knowing how to balance the big picture with the details is the key. Using ambiguous but positive adjectives only goes so far. The Trump descriptors like "huge, perfect, big, beautiful" are not always helpful.

READ ALL ABOUT IT...

- *Dealing with the press is a skill. Leaders need to know how to deal with all media including social media in order to deliver the intended message, although that still doesn't mean the desired messages will be heard.*

Call them fake, call them relentless, call them biased, call them fair, call them necessary but most of all, make sure when **they** call, you know how to deal with them. The media is the channel through which your world is influenced. Sometimes the treatment by the press is as critical as performance. Leadership's job is communicating to all audiences, and the press needs to be a part of the communication process. And be sure to be interesting enough that the press wants to follow you.

THINK ANYONE WILL NOTICE?

- *Personal style and appearance are always under scrutiny for leaders. What may seem incidental like a handshake, a haircut, the cut of a suit, or the length of a tie will draw attention if they are not the "norm".*

Yes, they always notice. A leader's appearance becomes a part of his or her brand. When it comes to Donald Trump, almost all of his decisions about his appearance are keeping with his brand of being an outsider. As his critics are quick to point out, his suits are too baggy, his ties are too long, his hats are too small, his skin is sort of orange, and his hair is "indescribable". Yet, he persists and as his policies and ideas are examined, all of his appearance discussions disappear because there are crazier things to discuss. Do something big and people will stop discussing your hair.

8

Judgment Is in the Eye of the Beholder

Judge Judy, where is your clarity when we need it? Judgment is about choosing the right thing to do. Judgment is about picking the best alternative, even when all the alternatives are bad. Good judgment is a commodity that will make a leader not just successful, but legendary. Any lack of judgment will lead to the penalty box.

SOME OF MY BEST FRIENDS...

- *When it comes to racism, there are not two sides to the story. Waffling about hate is not the way to go.*

Racism comes in many forms. Any form will and should get you fired. End of story. Any vacillation or subtle acceptance is still not OK. Why does this need repeating today? And the word "but" when inserted into a statement about race should never be necessary. As in, "Some of my best friends are Muslim, but..." Tacit recognition of hate groups is the same thing as supporting racism. Through words, deeds, or lack of works, leaders who are painted with any blush of racism will not last long.

NO GRAY AREA EXISTS

- *Why do I even have to mention this?*

Once labeled a racist, it is difficult to get out from under the brand so any leader should steer clear of any word or deed that will push him or her into that category. Phrases like "Go back to where you came from" are firmly in the category that will make the racist description come forward. Whether it be a racist joke or an offhand comment about slavery, any inclination of racism will be picked up and nothing good will happen as a result. Only words decrying racism are worthy of a leader. Anything else could and should get you fired.

WHAT, ARE YOU IN THE THIRD GRADE...?

- *Calling people names or making fun of them is immature, petty, and does not reflect the stature that a leader needs to manage and make good decisions.*

Ask yourself, what would (fill in the blank) do? For me, the blank might be filled in with names like Liam Neeson, James Bond, or Paul Newman. How would they handle themselves in a given situation? None of them would use a disparaging name or make fun of anyone with a disability. Imagine James Bond calling someone "Pocahontas" or "Lying Ted" or "Little Marco". (With a name like Moran, I continue to deal with a snickered switch of one letter and called Moron. It was not funny in the third grade and it is still not funny.)

ONE MAN'S CEILING IS ANOTHER MAN'S FLOOR

- *Someone else always has more money, more toys, and more friends. Enjoy what you have and don't boast about it.*

The lists of the richest, the most powerful, the hottest, the boldest, and the best under thirty years old can make us feel like we are losers. We are not. To compare your lot to others is to assign a life of striving for something that can't be reached. The social media sites don't help. Facebook and other sites are just more ways to make you feel bad about what we don't have. Stop paying attention. The self-help aisle in the bookstore is loaded with advice about being satisfied with what you have. Try it.

THIS COULD BE A PROBLEM...

- *When the spouse of one of your lieutenants calls your performance a "shit show" or a "green bin on fire", there could be trouble at home **and** in the office.*

Marriage is hard enough. Being a leader is hard enough. Being a spokesperson for a controversial leader is impossibly difficult. Why make it all even more onerous or even embarrassing. Lessons here could include choosing a spouse carefully, never marrying someone with a potty mouth, or explaining to one's spouse over dinner what your job is and how the real "shit show" may be sitting across from you at the dinner table. A supportive spouse is required to be successful. You can't fight battles at home and in the office.

ALL I DO IS WIN...

- *If you win, there is no need to be a mean bastard. After a victory is the time for pride and humility.*

You won! Get over it and get back to work. The win doesn't have to be an election or a game. Maybe you were promoted over someone else. Maybe your project team received the award. Remember who won the championship last year? Probably not. Think of that star high school athlete who still talks about those glory days. Boring. After winning is when the work in earnest begins.

GOD, COUNTRY, APPLE PIE

- *Certain things are sacred; to violate that sanctity is like stepping on a land mine.*

The flag, 9/11 victims, veterans, puppies, babies are not to be criticized. Freedom of speech aside, no criticism on certain subjects is ever welcome. A leader can take a stand, even an unpopular one, if there is a reason and logic behind the stand. Such an action can bring admiration and gravitas to the leader. But when it comes to criticizing war heroes or admired institutions or anything held dear, such criticism can be seen as a jealous act or at the very least, below the dignity of the leader. Let cherished sleeping dogs lie.

SINK OR SWIM MANAGEMENT CAN LEAD TO GREAT THINGS

- *When thrown in over your head learn how to swim as fast as you can.*

How many people know how to manage a major corporation or lead a country? It's a short list. As a result, almost all leaders learn on the job once appointed. We just hope the learning process isn't that long and major mistakes aren't made right away. A great leader will recognize the most important things that need to be done right away and bring in all the experts and thought leaders to help perform analysis and make decisions. Everyone brings a unique personality and distinct set of quirks and styles to leadership. That uniqueness will always be put to the test in early days when the leader is in over his or her head. Donald Trump never let on he was in over his head and brought his own style to the office. Learning curves are for others.

IF I SHOT YOU WHEN I WANTED, I'D BE OUT BY NOW

- *Threats are never useful. Or are they?*

Violence shouldn't be in the leader's toolbox. Even threats of violence don't belong there. But there are exceptions if you are Commander-in-Chief. Threatening foreign enemies is one thing, threatening people who don't support you is another. When threatened with being undermined as a leader, there are times when threats in turn may thwart being unseated. Threats of violence are not the way to do that.

I LOVE THE SMELL OF A "SHARPIE" IN THE MORNING

- *A "Sharpie" marker can be an important policy shaper.*

Who knew a Sharpie could be such a useful tool for a leader? A slash with a Sharpie can be emphatic, dramatic, and cast a spell of drama over an occasion not to mention the smell of something important about to happen. A Sharpie can create a signature that helps create a brand. What it cannot do is change what is already widely known and believed. A leader can use PowerPoint Presentations, Post-It Notes, a Sharpie, and all manner of charts to explain a point of view, and all of those tools can help with communications but doesn't alter or cover up the truth. BTW, when you write in bold with a Sharpie, others can read what you write and photograph it.

I DIDN'T KNOW YOU COULD SPEAK LATIN

- *A Quid Pro Quo can be a bargain with the devil.*

You scratch my back, I'll scratch yours can be a signal of love or a signal from the mafia that if you don't do something they want, you will die. When it comes to international diplomacy, it is often used too in trade agreements and in brokering deals. Brokering quids and quos with foreign powers to investigate political rivals is usually not a good thing to do if you want to avoid criticism or worse. Foreign Service Officers are not accustomed to such dealings and will not be your friend if they suspect such dealings. Just saying.

NEVER WASTE A CRISIS

- *Natural disasters can't be planned.*

Earthquakes, hurricanes, tornadoes, floods, and fires, there is no limit to the crazy events that seem to happen every week. Each one calls for leadership to give hope and solutions. Disasters are not a time for self-aggrandizement or empty promises. The opportunity to emerge as a leader during a crisis is unique and a leader should jump into that fray for good. For corporations, a crisis can include a security breach, a work injury, or a product problem and the same rules apply – jump into the fray. But only the President has the really big opportunity to alter the outcome of crisis recovery. The opportunity should not be wasted by not showing up or by making a callous comment or tossing paper towels around. Donald Trump has learned that lesson.

NEVER GOING BACK TO MY OLD SCHOOL

- *A leader should be proud of the alma mater. It's too late to change it.*

Look at anyone's obituary, and one of the first items listed is where the deceased attended college. For most of us, the college experience happened between the ages of eighteen and twenty-two, a time when we want to take a big bite out of the apple of experience. Regardless of what happened then and what might show up later that causes embarrassment, after graduation, you can't change where you went to school and it's way too late to try to change those grades. As a leader, you learned things along the way that were probably shaped by school experiences so be proud of that connection and make your alma mater proud.

CHEESEBURGER IN PARADISE

- *Each day, any leader can eat several breakfasts, catch a "coffee" or two, be invited to three lunches, and capped off by two dinners with colleagues or customers. Make the personal appearance but stay away from the cheese balls. Leadership and fast food is a bad combination that will make you gain weight and be less energetic.*

Leaders are sought after for their time, not the time spent in meetings but the time spent in more informal sessions – like any meal. It's the yin and yang of being accessible without getting fat. So the invitations roll in: "Can we grab a coffee? Can we do lunch soon? Can I buy you a drink? How about dinner sometime?" And that would be every day. The two solutions are obvious: Either say no or say yes but don't eat. Being so busy that you have to eat on the run is not any better. "On the run" means a steady diet of fast food that sends out the message of not being concerned about health (based on thousands of reports) and a lack of appreciation for leadership style.

PLAGUES, LOCUSTS, FLOODS, FIFTY CAR PILEUPS

- *Every crisis and disaster is different and comparing one to another is just as dangerous as the disaster.*

When you are in a crisis, it is the only one that counts and maybe you think it's the only one that ever existed. If your house burnt down in the California fires, you don't care if the floods in Houston were more devastating. All you care about is getting back to normal if it will ever exist again. A leader recognizes that what is important is what is happening now and making the appropriate actions. A leader shows empathy even if he or she has never had anything bad happen to them. Disasters are an opportunity for a leader, not a nuisance.

SORRY SEEMS TO BE THE HARDEST WORD

- *Say you're sorry when it is needed. Saying, "I never apologize" is not a sustainable position.*

The world is a better place when people say they are sorry when it is needed. Imagine someone cutting you off on the highway and instead of flipping the bird at you, the other driver mouths "I'm sorry" as he or she speeds away. Imagine a leader promising something that everyone knows is just not going to happen and finally says, "I'm sorry, but what I promised is just not going to happen. Let's move on". There are times when an apology does make things better. There are situations where a leader's apology is warranted. It is a sign of strength, not weakness. Apologies that are rare can be meaningful.

SHINY OBJECTS AND BUTTERFLIES ARE ALWAYS FLYING AROUND

- *Distractions always exist. In spite of the tendency to chase after every opportunity, focus on what is the most important.*

Most leaders agree that they spend the bulk of their time on unproductive activities. Instead of planning or operating, they tend to focus on problems, large and small, right in front of them. It was there, I had it in my grasp and then my text buzzed and the idea was lost forever. Focus, focus, focus wins the day.

LOOK AT IT THIS WAY...

- *Small acts matter. Never underestimate the signals that can be sent by scheduled choices, people choices, and seemingly inconsequential actions. Never throw paper towels to a group that is drowning.*

Leadership can sometimes be shown through small shows of humanity – time with children, playing with a dog, or singing a special song even if you can't sing. Leadership, or the lack of it, can be shown too by small acts of disregard for others. Never, ever seem callous to children, those with disabilities, dogs, war veterans, or those who are suffering from a tragedy. When you have a "listening session", really lesson, don't talk, especially about yourself.

IT REALLY ISN'T OVER UNTIL IT'S OVER

- *Declaring victory too soon can bite you in the butt.*

The oldest rule in the book is "don't stop running until you cross the finish line". In the leadership game that holds true as well. What seemed like a bad decision when first made might turn in different directions as that decision winds its way through the organization. Or, what was once dramatic soon becomes matter of course. Moving an embassy from one city to another or changing regulations may garner headlines one day but the next day may seem to make sense. But in all cases, claiming victory before the final period or the final vote is never a good plan, no matter the score.

SECOND OPINION NOT REQUIRED

- *The family smell test is always accurate.*

Any boorish behavior that you wouldn't want your mom or children subjected to is bullying. No need for a legal opinion. Anyone in power is subject to a strict scale because almost any provocative move can be seen as bullying. Is calling someone a derogatory name bullying? Probably. Is threatening people bullying? Again, probably. Are putting sanctions on a weaker nation bullying? Yes. Leaders need to know the power of the position and when that power can be exercised for desired results. There is a difference, and an effective leader knows which is which. In general, a bully is not the leader people like but the actions may get what the leader wants.

AT LEAST WE'RE ALL WRONG TOGETHER

- *It may take longer and all the options may need to be explored but building consensus with the team is almost always worth the effort.*

The process of consensus can be tedious. Everyone wants to be heard, even the guy who snores through most meetings will wake up when it's his turn. If the leader doesn't care about reaching consensus, then the effort is a total waste of time. If there is no time for consensus, then hope that the leader is using judgment and makes the best decisions. Not all voices are the same. Sometimes consensus means that a group decides to do something that no one really wants to do.

I USED TO BE SOMEBODY, NOW I AM SOMEBODY ELSE

- *Skills from business don't always transfer to other sectors.*

It's a belief that has been around since Henry Ford: if only government and not-for-profit organizations would adopt principles from the business world they would be more effective. If only they weren't so stubborn. Or worse is the belief that the people in government or education are not smart enough to adopt business principles and that's why nothing works there. Think, "Those who can, do; those who can't, teach". Some processes and ways of thinking from business do adapt to other worlds. Some things, not so much. The skills one builds in the business world also may transfer, or not. Like translating a language, there are nuances and some people are better at making the transition than others.

ALL THE KING'S HORSES AND
ALL THE KING'S MEN

- *Building security walls are expensive and controversial. Who wants to work behind a wall?*

Walls don't always work. Someone is always falling off of them, digging under them, hitting them with new weapons, or climb ing them with crazy fantasy figures who will not die. Walls are a simple solution to complex problems. From the outside walls do work in sending the message that "this place is private and you are not welcome, survivors will be shot". Country clubs can send out that message. From the inside of the wall the message is, "We are special and don't come in". That is, unless you are inside a prison wall. Leaders understand both the physical implications of walls and the powerful messages that walls can deliver and not take actions on walls lightly. The power of a wall is well understood by Mr. Trump.

RECEIVING A SUBPOENA USUALLY MEANS YOU NEED TO SHOW UP

- *Unless you have a big batch of lawyers, I wouldn't test this request.*

The receipt of a subpoena usually means that you will have to do something that you don't want to do. Ignoring a subpoena will be interpreted that there is something to hide. Lawyers can delay things, but it is usually best to do what needs to be done and move on. Depositions and subpoenas don't go away and they can become like that parking ticket that you refuse to pay and the penalty just keeps increasing. Lawyers going back and forth constantly with a myriad of suits to settle and deal with are perceived as the leader stonewalling and wasting time and money.

IS THIS MY LAST CHANCE?

- *Best indicator of future behavior is past behavior.*

Bankruptcies? Divorces? Skrimping on paying vendors? Growing companies? Doing complicated deals with international groups? The research is consistent that, by far, the best predictor of future performance is past performance. The same is true for behaviors. People may promise to change and we might hope they do but the results in this category are grim. What you saw is what you will get. As a leader, people were willing to look some of Donald Trump's questionable behavior in the belief that he would get things done and put the United States back on a positive track.

WHO DOESN'T LOVE A PARADE?

- *A show of pride, patriotism, and community is the big idea.*

Parades are almost always a celebration. Even funeral parades are a celebration of a life now gone. The only reasons not to have one are costs, logistics, or if the parade is only to serve one's ego. A parade can be a time to rejoice about all the good things that the organization or nation has going for it. Donald Trump knows this simple fact and would have a parade every day if he could. Let the parades happen.

SOMEDAY, JUST NOT TODAY

- *The event of the day may be what needs to be handled, not what you planned.*

Today was the day to meet with the cub scouts, have a leisurely lunch, and do some planning. Not too bad. Except there is a green bin fire in Ohio and an unidentified missile in the air somewhere and the Israelis are having another election issue. It's a new day, but not the one we wanted. Making choices between the urgent, the critical, and the important is part of the daily routine for the leader. Judgment and gut feeling are not the same. Donald Trump needs to understand the difference.

IT WAS JUST PLAYING AROUND

- *Discussing sex or politics at work is not recommended. Discussing sex in politics is hard to avoid.*

Most behaviors are open to interpretation but some are not. Looking at pornography while on the job is not open to interpretation. You will get fired. "Just playing around" to a man can mean assault to a woman. And if that's the case, you will be fired. Anything sexual in discussion or deed is an activity that is so open to interpretation that no one wants to hear about it. Or, talking about it will only get you in trouble especially if you will ever be nominated to the Supreme Court. Leaders don't discuss sexual exploits or ever do anything that will now or later be open to interpretation.

9

Not Quite Right (NQR) – Really?

It's not a pleasant feeling when your gut tells you something is "not quite right" (NQR). Maybe you left the stove burner on, maybe you left your keys in your car, maybe there is a "look" in your partner's eyes. Whatever it is, it makes you uncomfortable and sometimes you can't quite put your finger on it. We can feel the same way about our leaders. Maybe it's pattern recognition when a leader reminds you of your crazy uncle who shows up drunk at every holiday. Or maybe it's intuition that is telling your brain, "I don't know about that…". That NGR feeling is often something that is true and should be embraced.

━━━━━━━━━

I HEAR YOU KNOCKING BUT I'M NOT HERE

- *Stonewalling is a tactic of delay, dismiss, and deflect that can work.*

Not doing anything can be a strategy. The problem is not doing anything can result in things going sideways and being set up for more criticism. Refusal to testify, refusal to provide documents, ignoring subpoenas, and missing meetings are all part of stonewalling and all ways to prevent forward progress. The Trump administration is expert at stonewalling and not playing into adversaries' agendas. His own agenda may not move forward but neither does anyone else's agenda. And for Trump, while stonewalling, his agenda doesn't go backward either. It can be an effective technique to go nowhere and stay there.

HINDSIGHT CAN BE BLURRY

- *Criticizing one's predecessor is not a formula for success; especially if he or she is now or was popular. Look forward, not backward.*

Leaders are often more popular once they stop leading. Why not? They are no longer doing any damage (think George W. Bush). Better to understand those who went before you and the issues they had to deal with and empathize, don't criticize. And who cares what happened before in the context of a new leader? Criticizing a predecessor will seem like you are setting yourself up to be blameless in any decision you make and that's not the way it works. Regardless of what happened then, what is happening now and how you handle it is on your watch. It's all about the future now and what you will do to make it better. Continuously disparaging a predecessor or a vanquished rival seems weak. Get over it.

ITS ONLY FOUR YEARS...

- *Organizations can survive unpopular or ineffective leaders. The answer to the question, "How much damage can he or she do?" is usually not all that much. There are exceptions.*

The established belief is that institutions can withstand a poor or erratic performer until someone or some group comes to their senses and the leader is removed. People in many organizations just wait out leaders in the knowledge that he or she will soon be gone, and things will get back to "normal". However, there are cases where the damage that a leader can inflict is so great that an intervention is needed before the damage is irreversible. Donald Trump has changed the leadership thinking as to how much damage or change a leader can induce in four years. The measures of damage or accomplishments may never be the same. The Google credo of "Do No Harm" should apply to all leaders.

THE "PERMANENT RECORD" DOES EXIST

- *What happens in Las Vegas does not stay in Las Vegas. It never did. Every action and sin is subject to later review.*

Maybe it happened in high school at a house party where you drank a lot of beer. You like beer. Maybe it happened in college at that sorority party where people were taking lots of photos. Maybe it happened at the corporate off-site at the after after party with tequila involved. Whatever happened, if there were victims, witness, or, worse, photos, you could be in trouble down the road no matter how long the road. The best solution is to not do anything crazy in the first place. If it's too late, say prayers and forget the nomination to the Supreme Court. It might be time to burn the old yearbooks. Of course, like many things that don't apply to the rest of us, Donald Trump can work around his *Permanent Record* with aplomb.

YOU CAN'T MAKE THIS STUFF UP

- *The convergence of wild personalities, social media, and constant news cycles might make us shake our heads in horror. It's the challenge of change.*

Everyone agrees change is good for everyone else. "They" always need to change. When you are the President, pretty much any change is going to be greeted with applause as well as venom. This has been true whether you are George Washington or Donald Trump or any President in between. Yet, the sheer volume of changes introduced by Donald Trump and the way in which the media covered every one of his changes has made our heads spin. Some leaders try to change a thousand things in the hopes that ten of them will stick. Among all of the commotion, real change **is** happening on leadership thinking, acceptable behavior and attitudes. Whether or not you like the changes is up to you.

IT WORKED IN THE LAB

- *Practice sessions that go poorly means that the real session will be a train wreck too.*

Miracles might happen in sports and in theater, but rehearsals are good indicators of what a leader will face in the organizational arena. If an appearance is a half-hearted or an apology is reticent, it will be seen as lackluster and not sincere. If the debate preparation is a disaster, the debate will be a disaster. If there is no preparation or practice session, the chances are even higher that nothing good will happen in real time. The pros know that practice and rehearsing makes any performance better. All leaders know early in a career that "winging it" is a risk. Spontaneous is one thing that can build a leadership reputation. Conversely, a leader who is ill prepared will be seen as just that – ill prepared. Donald Trump has flashes of brilliance at both.

HELL HATH NO FURY...

- *Interfering with the relationship between parents and children is not a legacy to pursue. Emotions can overrule policy any day.*

The only fist fight I ever witnessed on an airplane was when a passenger told another passenger to "make that baby shut up!" Fisticuffs ensued. Even though every parent knows that no child is perfect, every parent's child is above criticism from others. The act of separating children from parents is beyond the pale when it comes to criticism. Everyone agrees that immigration policy needs to be reformed, but the real issue was obscured when the visuals of children crying for their parents were presented. It's a lesson that even Donald Trump has taken to heart. Families are to stay together, even if they are in the "No Man's Land" of waiting for asylum.

SINCE I WON THE LOTTERY, I HAVE NEW FRIENDS

- *Keep long-term allies and friends. Be wary of those who want to be new friends.*

New leaders attract new friends. New friends are not always the best and most loyal friends although some might prove to be the friends you need in your new position. Leaders need to be on red alert when building a team. The team should be one that is not only loyal but competent and experienced in the places they are most needed. If there is any doubt, about the intentions of any new team member, it's better to act early. The world is littered with financially ruined rock stars and athletes who created a posse only to learn that the posse was a group of hangers-on who were along for the ride. Presidents need to exercise the same cautions but not TOO much.

ARE ICELAND OR BELGIUM AVAILABLE?

- *Big ideas are the heroin of great leaders.*

The United States has always considered buying property from other countries. It is the art of the deal. Consider the Louisiana Purchase or Seward's Folly when he bought Alaska or the big deal with Mexico that brought California, New Mexico, and a few others into the Union. The idea of buying another country like Greenland may not be as far-fetched as it at first appears. Why not propose it? Big ideas attract attention and discussion. Big ideas make little problems seem even smaller. Big ideas create a legacy. The most satisfied leaders are the ones that dream of big ideas and bring them to fruition. Big idea leaders are not crazy although it may seem that way at first. Donald Trump trades in big ideas, implementable or not, but the ideas garner attention.

TERMS ARE THIRTY DAYS

- *Paying vendor's bills will pay dividends over time. Don't screw people. Period.*

The world is full of people who don't pay their bills. Most are hunted down and humiliated by bill collectors. Some watch their car get towed away in the dark of night. Some get away without paying their bills, but not many. Usually, people don't pay their bills because they don't have any money. Those people who don't pay usually wish they could pay their bills because their lives are miserable from the phone calls from bill collectors. There are others who don't pay bills, especially from vendors because they consider it a contest, and if they can get away without paying the bills, then they win. Not paying bills when you can is cheating and no one likes cheaters. It's not a contest. Paying bills is the right thing to do.

BEING ON CONSTANT "RED ALERT" STATUS IS GOOD DEFENSE BUT EXHAUSTING

- *Accusations of "being crazy" always require a strong response.*

When those around you use the word "intervention" in order to prevent you from doing anything rash, maybe the pressure is getting to you. Interventions are commonly used for drug issues, eating disorders, addictions, or for those who may do bodily harm or act out in a senseless way. When opponents put you in one of those categories, it's time for a reset to assure the world that there is no need for any intervention. "Intervention" required is a damning assessment of a leader's performance implying irrational and out-of-control behavior. Slightly less damning is the phrase, "I pray for him/her" implying that only prayers can save us. Prayers could also mean the leader just needs help from special places. Donald Trump has lots of prayers for him.

SOMETIMES IT IS ROCKET SCIENCE

- *Skills from business don't always transfer to other sectors.*

Somewhere right now someone is sitting at a conference table saying, "When I was at IBM..." (or Intel or General Electric or, you fill in the blank corporation). The implication is that someone knows better because they used to be in the business world and "this is the way things should be done". Wrong! Some business skills apply in the not-for-profit world or government world but not all. The world of helping people or setting policy is different from the world of generating profits. Challenge the experts but listen. As one President is finding out, doing a "deal" with a foreign leader in exchange for a favor may work in business but not in diplomacy.

IN CASE OF EMERGENCY, BREAK GLASS

• *If everything is an emergency, nothing is an emergency.*

Maybe for any US President everything every day is an emergency. The striking photos of Presidents taken as they enter office compared with the photo of when they leave office suggest the wear and tear such a leadership role demands. But maybe, just maybe, not everything is an emergency. Impeachment hearings are an emergency, nuclear showdowns are emergencies, hurricanes and fires are emergencies and require leadership of the highest quality. Treating everything as a crisis will confuse people like "crying wolf". Leaders can differentiate the urgent from the critical from the routine and act accordingly. Donald Trump is the exception in that he thrives on emergencies and has no lack of willingness to create them.

YOU NEED TO CALM DOWN

- *Not everything is a crisis and worthy of attention.*

Managing emotions is a leadership skill. When people seem to be after you it's even harder to manage those emotions. A leader can check emotions as necessary to make the right decisions. Impulsive decisions based on emotions will almost always get a leader into trouble. Putting emotions aside is a difficult skill to develop but critical to success. And tweeting when emotional may be a way to get even but may create a situation that you will later regret. As in other impulsive actions that can get us into trouble, better to wait until the morning to decide what reaction is required, if any. It's like drunk dialing your boss or old girlfriend at 2:00 am. Even for Donald Trump, the news cycle can wait.

I DIDN'T DO ANYTHING WRONG

- *Impeachment is complicated, distracting, and takes a long time but may be worth it when crimes are involved.*

Usually a leader knows when it's time to go and any leader wants to exit gracefully with recognition dinners and smiles. Knowing that the time has come could be based on polls, performance, a gut feeling, weariness, boredom or people with pitchforks, and flaming torches at the gate. Or, regardless of all the signals, sometimes the leader wants to stay in spite of all the signals to the contrary. So the battle for power ensues. Performance is in the eye of the beholder. So is malfeasance. No leader wants to be driven from office, any leader wants to ensure a positive legacy rather than being known as the person who was fired. For a President, impeachment is the ultimate in disgrace and will always lead to a long, drawn out fight until there is nothing left worth fighting for.

SITTING DOWN IS THE NEW SMOKING

- *Photos taken while you are sitting down makes you look short.*

The handshake is important, ask any career coach about interview impressions. Donald Trump has made the handshake a symbol of power with other leaders as each one sits in a chair at an angle to his chair. Are his hands small? Who cares because he uses that shake to send a message of dominance. Besides, recent research suggests that sitting down all day is bad for your health. Stand up, get the blood circulating, do a dance, and face the music. You will feel better.

YOU DON'T PULL THE MASK OFF
THE OLD LONE RANGER

- *Protocols matter. Breaking them can cause embarrassment of world wars.*

Sacred cows don't become sacred overnight. Traditions are developed over time and often out of respect for something or someone. Walking in front of the Queen of England is one of those protocols not to be stepped on. But some traditions can hold a leader back from making progress, and in those cases, the sacred cows need to be shot. In other cases, if following the protocol is going to cause a disruption that is bigger than the protocol, maybe it's time for a change. If the Super Bowl champions don't want to attend an event in their honor, don't have the event. Leaders need to know which protocols will enhance their ability to lead and which ones will have people wondering about judgment. Donald Trump is the master of shooting sacred cows and some cows needed to be shot.

HOW DO YOU LIKE ME NOW?

- *Never underestimate the power of a vengeful billionaire.*

They made fun of Donald Trump. It happened at a dinner in Washington D.C. and he was embarrassed. He got even. Regardless of whether or not he ever wanted to be President, he became one and the leader of the free world and, while he's at it, the most famous person in the world. His ability to rebound and assume a role for which he is ill prepared is unprecedented.

NOW WHAT?

- *When all seems lost, maybe it is.*

Be realistic. Sometimes the captain needs to abandon ship. When you can see the villagers coming toward the castle with pitchforks and torches, it is time to explore options and "as is" may not be an option. The villagers mean business and the business is you and your leadership style. A key part of leadership is knowing when it is time to go and to let someone who may be more effective take over. It is not an easy decision to make. Maybe it's a resignation or a retirement or an "of counsel" role. Think what is best for the country or the organization and then make the decision. Listening to congressional testimony may provide clues too.

10

Personal Traits, Habits, Ticks, and Quirks

A leader's persona is a package from hair to socks. The persona includes spouses, children, sports, eating preferences, drinking habits, and all the rest. In the parlance of social media, the persona is all the direct and indirect things that build a personal brand. Millions of little decisions build the brand, and every leader should pay attention to the brand.

WHEN THE DOG CATCHES THE CAR

- *Be careful what you try for you might get it.*

No one is more surprised than the dog when the teeth lock around that rear bumper. Now what? The same holds true when seeking a leadership role or even a job. Sometimes you get things that you really never wanted, but here you are. At this point the leader can say, "I was only kidding, I was just testing the waters, I don't want the job, I just wanted to prove that I could get it, good luck", but that hardly ever happens. Instead, most will say, "Why not? I'll give it a try and see what happens". That's when things get tricky and some leaders realize they are totally unprepared for the new role. Sometimes a fresh perspective can make things better; sometimes not. The transition time into the new role can be brutal as Donald Trump well knows.

THE MIRROR DOESN'T LIE

- *Self-awareness is a virtue for leaders.*

Self-awareness is more than understanding one's strengths and weaknesses. Knowing yourself means understanding your own style, motives, emotions, and the will to get things done and implement strategies. A leader who is not self-aware will not understand the impact that every decision large and small will have on the organization. A self-aware leader will think of reversing the lenses so that he or she can see what others see and make adjustments accordingly based on the answer to the question, "Is that who I want to be?" Donald Trump may look in the mirror, but the self-awareness quotient is either incredibly high or lacking. There is no middle ground here.

LOOK FOR THE BARE NECESSITIES

- *Thoughtful is a trait that will be appreciated by those around you.*

A new book regarding business management and leadership is published each and every day. We have *Leadership Lessons from Attila the Hun* as well as *Leading from Behind*. It is difficult to assess which leadership book sets the tone for Donald Trump, if any. He is writing his own real-time book. Rather, everyone else, including me, is writing leadership books about him trying to figure him out. After reading many, many leadership books, I do know that a trait that others value in a leader is the ability to be thoughtful. A word that is rarely associated with President Trump is "thoughtful".

DO YOU HEAR WHAT I HEAR?

- *Listening is an underrated skill for leaders. The best leaders are the best listeners.*

A leader doesn't claim, "I hear you". Uttering that phrase alone is not listening. A leader might say, "I hear you and this is what we are going to do (or not do) about it". Whether the issue is food in the break room, employee parking, climate change, or gun control, a response one way or another means listening took place. Effective leaders listen and then act. Even better, a leader states, "I looked at the data, I listened to the experts and constituents, and based on that analysis, here is what we are going to do…" It would be a great day in leadership annals when Donald Trump uttered that sentence.

SMILE LIKE YOU MEAN IT

- *Smile. A sense of humor can make you more approachable, more human, more interesting – more successful. Cultivate a sense of humor. Smile. Laugh at yourself.*

Who doesn't want to be around smiling people? A smile can reflect pleasure with a job well done or joy in seeing someone that you care for or a sense of confidence. Stay away from smirks, which have the opposite effect. A leader needs to show humanity, needs to open the heart when appropriate, and what easier way to do it than with a smile. Think of a leader that you admire and I bet a sense of humor and a smile is involved.

IS MINE BIGGER THAN YOURS?

- *Never be critical or boast about the perks that come with management.*

Leadership does have its perks that could include everything from a private bathroom to ready use of a Boeing 747. Most perks are an unimaginable luxury for the man or woman slugging it out for a paycheck every week. Don't complain about the free food in the executive dining room or brag about the motorcade that you require any time you move. It's not about you, it's about the job. Leaders take nothing for granted. Nothing lasts forever and leaders know it.

STORMING OUT OF MEETINGS WILL ALWAYS MAKE FOR SHORT MEETINGS

- *"You are wasting my time" is a strong message.*

Anyone in a large organization will probably agree that there are too many meetings. There can be meetings to eliminate so many meetings. People usually like the doughnuts or whatever food is served at the meeting so they will attend. If the most important person in attendance storms out, the meeting is over. If the most important person who is supposed to be there doesn't show, the meeting is over before it starts. Meetings can be productive and usually have a purpose. Storming out of meetings is one way to eliminate them. Donald Trump has the "storming out" part down to a science when things aren't going well.

HE MAY BE AN ASSHOLE BUT
HE'S OUR ASSHOLE

- *The "No Asshole Rule" only applies until the asshole gets a following.*

There can be no doubt that some of our leaders are assholes. In the vernacular, that means someone who is inconsiderate, arrogant, selfish, mean, and ornery among other things. Regardless of those traits, some will follow and believe in such a character because he (an asshole is always a man, there are other descriptive words for women) gets things done. We tolerate assholes when the team cannot operate without them but that tolerance doesn't last long because teams realize they can do just fine without the jerk. No one needs to tolerate the asshole.

YOU PROBABLY THINK THIS IS ALL ABOUT YOU

- *Ego can be a leadership killer – don't believe your own public relations.*

Confidence in a leader is a requirement and a leader's healthy ego is part of that confidence. That is, until the ego gets so big that an egotistical jerk emerges. It can be a fine line. The GOATs, the Greatest of All Times, rarely proclaim themselves to hold that crown. A self-aware leader will know when the fine line between self-assured and self-aggrandizing is crossed. Most would say that Donald Trump crossed that line early and often and is still on the wrong side of the line. If the results match the ego, the leader can be great. If not, the leader is the narcissist.

SMUCKERS, FORBES, KOHLER, FORD

- *Putting your own name on everything is an efficient way to be memorialized*

Washington and Lincoln didn't put their names on their houses. It probably never crossed their minds. Others, from industry placed their names on jars of jelly, magazines, automobiles, and toilet bowls with good results. If one has the money and the clout, why not put the family name on an enterprise? The only problem is that when things don't go right, those named places and things could become the symbol of what is wrong with one's leadership style. Ego aside, sometimes it does make sense for a leader to use the family name in branding. President Trump recognized the power of the brand and used it early and often.

I AM NOT RACIST BUT...

- *People have radar when it comes to racism or misogyny and can always spot an offender.*

Like it or not, discrimination is a part of what makes us tick. We all respond to different people and actions in different ways based on lots of factors including where we were when growing up. The key is to turn the discrimination into positives. Phrases like "some of my best friends are black or gay..." or "I am color blind" do not help and send up signals that leaders may not want to send. Recognition of racism is seen through performance, not words. Take a look at the comments, Cabinet appointments and actions of President Trump and decide for yourself.

WHEN I WAS YOUR AGE

- *Standards change.*

Those messy divorces or that DUI arrest record that could be career killers no longer matter. Probably. A President who has been twice divorced, through several bankruptcies, doesn't affiliate much with a religion and has been fodder for the tabloids for years has changed that set of standards. In many ways he has cleaned the way too for diverse leaders who have struggled. As in, if we can elect someone with that kind of history, we can appoint people with other kinds of unique past. What matters is performance, real or imagined. Standards have changed and Donald Trump has had a lot to do with that change.

I AM EXHAUSTED

- *Age doesn't matter but stamina does.*

You cannot be a navy fighter pilot when you are over twenty-seven years old. Or begin a fire fighting career after thirty years old. There are no such age limits for leaders but people do slow down. Leadership is difficult, demanding work both physically and mentally. Think of the demands each day when any leader gets out of bed. A leader like Donald Trump who is in a battle each day with the Democrats and fighting impeachment as well as dealing with other countries, friend or foe. I don't know how he has the strength to get out of bed. Is it a wonder how he does it given his age? It is exhausting to watch but give him credit for having stamina. Many wish he would stay in bed all day. Stamina is a requirement for leaders, the country club management style is from the last century.

IT'S DIFFICULT TO TRAVEL WITH GOLF CLUBS

- *International travel is not about golf courses.*

Talk about bulky and awkward. Many of us have all tried it and failed. Carrying golf clubs to business trips means you are going to play golf, not do business, or at least that's what everyone will think when they see you get out of the car with the clubs. Golf clubs are hard to hide, even on Air Force One. If not in Air Force One, you will get caught at the baggage pickup area. Everyone will see you. Unless you are the President, better to rent clubs when you get there and get the chance to play. Or, make the decision that the trip is about golf and don't feel guilty or decide this is about work and leave the clubs at home. It's difficult to do both.

THAT WAS YOUR FIRST MISTAKE

- *Not admitting a mistake when everyone knows it is out there is a mistake.*

"It takes a big person to admit their mistake" is a bromide often heard about leaders. Nonetheless, leaders hate to admit they ever made a mistake. One President in particular never admits mistakes and never apologizes. Even his most ardent supporters will acknowledge that he has made mistakes a time or two along the way but no apology ever happened. Should the leader show a little vulnerability by admitting mistakes or show strength by ignoring mistakes? Depends on the situation some would say, but most would say that leaders need to own up to mistakes to communicate the recognition that a mistake was made and it won't happen again. Mistakes happen. It is not a sign of weakness to acknowledge one.

YOUR MOTHER WEARS COMBAT BOOTS

- *Every slight, criticism, or compliment does not require a response.*

It can be a cycle that never ends and a big waste of time. Responding to criticism may ignite creativity in a leader, but it is not worth the trouble. A good leader will have supporters and detractors and we all are sensitive to criticism. We can have one hundred positive comments but that one slight will be the one we focus on and respond to. Better to get on with leading than calling others names. However, a public name-calling fight will always garner attention and if that's what you want go ahead. Donald Trump knows that calling people names will get a headline although at someone else's expense.

WHAT'S WRONG WITH YOU? HOW STUPID CAN YOU BE?

- *Calling anyone demeaning names will make others shudder.*

Awkward! Watching others quarrel or disparage each other will always make others cringe. It's embarrassing for everyone. Name-calling is bullying. Assigning nicknames, even with good intentions, can be a more subtle way of treating others in a demeaning way. Leader and bully shouldn't be used in the same sentence. It is not in the leader's best interest to resort to name-calling. Ever.

NOT EVERYONE CAN DANCE WITH THE STARS

- *Boring can be a respected trait in a leader.*

Former athletes do it. Former television stars do it. Former rock stars do it. Former dog trainers do it. They all appear on the TV show *Dancing with the Stars*. Should former high-ranking politicians do it? The jury is out, but it makes me shudder to watch former cabinet-level people on any reality show. The journey of going from setting nuclear policy to doing the Rhumba and submitting yourself to a TV voting public might be questionable. A certain weight and dignity goes with leadership that should not be tarnished. A leader should think about the first sentence that will be published in his or her obituary. Appearing on a reality show and getting voted off in early ballots may not be the desired obituary opening. Donald Trump, please don't go on *Dancing with the Stars* when you are out of office. Please.

IF I ONLY KNEW THEN WHAT I KNOW NOW

- *Even though you are the leader, you may not be the smartest person in the room. Pretending to be doesn't fool anyone.*

You can't be an expert in everything. You can't say, "No one knows more about drones, military tactics, Russian history, oceanography or flux capacitors (fill in the blank) than me" and get away with it. Effective leaders surround themselves with experts so that they don't have to know everything about everything. It's better to admit being on a steep learning curve than crash and burn from looking ignorant. Bad decisions result when you claim to be smart about something and you are not. Leading and learning are close relatives. Very smart people are the leader's best friends and should be close to the person making big decisions. As someone who has never held public office, Mr. Trump needs those very smart people around him.

MANAGEMENT IS NOT LIKE A BOX OF CHOCOLATES

- *Be the same person every day. People don't want to guess who they are dealing with.*

Like Forrest Gump said, "Life is like a box of chocolates. You never know what you're going to get". But the leader should not be like a box of chocolates. When the staff is not sure who will show up on any given day, it keeps them on their toes. If the monster shows up, it will be a long day. Or, will the nice person show up who asks about everyone's well-being, it will be a happy day, or should be. Always being "on guard" is stressful. To his credit, Donald Trump seems to be the same every day. You may not like the way he is every day, but at least he is consistent.

WHAT'S SOMEONE LIKE YOU DOING IN A PLACE LIKE THIS?

- *Pornography is not your friend. Nothing good will happen to you by hanging around with adult entertainers.*

It's not about being judgmental. It's not about being a Puritan. It's about lack of judgment. People make choices to be in the sex industry and that is their prerogative. (Sex trafficking and other criminal acts are an exception.) Adult entertainers do it for money, they are not the friend of any leader, they are adult entertainers. It's just not a good practice for leaders to hang around with hookers. What you did, when, how, and with whom will always be a subject that will garner interest in a part of your life you may not want to discuss. Too many examples of ruined careers in all walks of life include the two words, "sex worker". Donald Trump has proven himself to be Mr. Teflon in this regard because accusations don't stick. Nonetheless, he has changed the standard of appropriate behaviors for a leader.

THE BEST THING ABOUT GOLF IS A MULLIGAN

- *Business is still conducted over a golf game. Unless you are the leader and like bicycling or racquetball or basketball or another sport.*

In most parts of life or leadership, there are no do-overs. As much as many would like to have, a Brexit do-over or an election do-over or a love affair do-over, the Mulligan only exists in golf. Maybe that's why so many leaders love the game of golf; they would like to have a do-over in all parts of life but no such luck. Mulligans or not, so much business is still conducted over extracurricular activities that a leader needs to pick one and be good enough at it to invite others. Whether its sailing, drinking, rock climbing, or playing bridge, schmoozing still matters and to think otherwise keeps you out of leadership. There is no better schmoozer than Donald Trump.

BECAUSE YOU'VE GOT TO HAVE FRIENDS

- *Relationships matter more than money. The quality of your relationships will define you as a person and a leader.*

Who doesn't want others to cheer for them? What leader doesn't want others to rejoice at organizational and personal success? The relationships that are developed through professional activity should last a lifetime. If you want to know who is coming to your funeral, it will be family, college friends, neighbors, and, if you are a beloved leader, lots of friends from work days. Think about that. Think about Donald Trump and his relationships and who will turn up at his big party.

WHAT GOES AROUND REALLY DOES COME AROUND

- *The Walt Disney movies don't lie. Good guys win in the end.*

It may take a while, it may even only be in heaven or hell but the bromide about going and coming around is true. Take solace, the examples of bad leaders losing in disgrace in the end are legion. It may not seem so in the short run but it happens. Trump haters are waiting for it to happen. Trump lovers believe that there was no "going around" in the first place. Donald Trump believes he is doing the right thing and that he will win, no matter. For most leaders, life is better not to be subjected to this equation. Be fair and just from the start.

IF YOU DON'T KNOW A BULLY, YOU ARE ONE

- *Bullying is pushing people around wherever and whoever they are.*

Every one of us remembers being bullied because everyone of us has been the victim of the unfortunate practice. It may have happened in school, at work, or in the family, bullying is all around us. Bullying is a mean action and hurts emotionally and probably physically. We cheer for the person who finally confronts the bully and wins the day. Leaders are in a unique position to act as a bully or to prevent bullying. Condemning bullying at the same time that bullying is occurring means that you are a bully. If you have to ask if this is bullying, it is. Getting things done is important but not if there are dead bodies along the way.

WHAT DID MOTHER TERESA REALLY DO ANYWAY?

- *Criticism of beloved people will make you look small*

Just don't do it. Speak highly of others as much as you can. Some people are not to be questioned, it's a waste of a leader's emotional currency and that currency needs to be saved. Why get into a fight over whether a POW is brave or not? By in large, no one wants to be captured by the enemy and does their heroic best to survive. There are plenty of people who deserve criticism like mass shooters and other criminals. Let the venom flow there.

UNLESS YOU ARE TIGER WOODS

- *Playing golf every day is seen as not doing your job. Even if you are.*

Work is work. Golf is golf. Sure, business can be transacted on the golf course, but it seems more likely that golf is more about driving around in a cart, drinking beer, and swinging a club, not about presenting policy changes or new initiatives that will make the country better. I like golf and I like work, but I find it difficult to mix the two. The general perception is that anyone playing golf is taking the day off. Taking a lot of days off leads to the perception that you are not doing your job even if you own the golf club and you are playing golf with the president of another country. While the leader is keeping score of the golf game, everyone else is keeping track of how many times the leader played golf.

FLATTERY CAN GET YOU EVERYWHERE

- *Playing to an ego can turn into an effective love fest.*

Egos are a powerful part of any leader's makeup. In most cases, the ego is what contributed to his or her success. Some egos have no limits and can border on hubris. Most egos can find equilibrium between confidence and empathy. Some cannot and let the ego takeover and succumb to compliments and the "you're doing a great job" battery of comments. When others know that flattery will get them everywhere, it becomes a constant and can blind any leader to what is true and what is not. Others will take advantage of a leader who can succumb to the river of flattery that will pump up the ego. Effective leaders see through fake flattery and ignore it. The "Greatest President since Abraham Lincoln" likes flattery and heaps it on himself. It has worked for a lifetime for him.

FUTURE'S SO BRIGHT I NEED MY SHADES

• *Nothing is gained by dwelling on past victories or opponent's problems.*

Memories are short when it comes to leadership. Leadership is about what is happening now and in the future, not what happened before. Plus, former leaders tend to develop an aura of the good old days, no matter how bad they were at the time. Note that George W. Bush is popular again. Going back to dredge up what past leaders did or didn't do is not time well spent and can make a leader look jealous or petty. Donald Trump needs to discuss his plans more than he needs to criticize any former leader.

MIRROR, MIRROR ON THE WALL

• *Results count more than appearance.*

Everyone on the Titanic looked good. Dancing and partying were all that mattered right until the ship sunk. And still everyone looked good. For a leader, it does matter how you look – the hairstyle, the clothes, the whole package. As President Obama learned, the color and style of tan suit will be parsed infinitum. All will be forgiven or ignored, however, based on accomplishing goals or achieving results or if there are just bigger things to talk about. No one is discussing President Trump's appearance during impeachment hearings, but they are waiting for a sartorial mistake to jump on. Trump has managed the world away from his appearance.

A WHITE SPORTS COAT AND
A PINK CARNATION

- *Bring attention to signature things that you want to be part of your brand, like green socks or a pencil thin mustache.*

Cartoonists will always zero in on traits that standout whether it be big ears, big teeth, gaps in teeth, weight, or hairstyles. A dark suit, white shirt, long red tie, and an interesting hair style can be a trait too. Johnny Cash wore black every day. Creating your own brand is more important than ever today. Make it a brand that you are proud of and you can live up to. Otherwise as a leader, people will create your brand and it may not be one you like. Think "Hacksaw Al" or "the Dragon Lady". Donald Trump's brand as a leader is complex but carefully orchestrated. It works for him.

11

Making Deals Is an Art, a Science, and a Mystery

It's one thing to do a deal between two companies that want to merge. It's another thing to do a deal with two countries that have been fighting since the Middle Ages. It's not the same, or is it? Deals are difficult whether it be with a child who won't go to bed or a belligerent adversary. Some people are really good at making deals, and they are usually the rich people. Like many others, I wish I was one of them.

ANSWER HAZY, TRY AGAIN...

- *"Agree in concept" is a long way from "I agree". An MOU is a long way from "it is done". A signed agreement needs to include specifics, next steps, thresholds, gateways, goals, actions, or something to point to that connotes progress. "Deal or no deal" is a misnomer.*

Killing agreements is one thing, reaching agreements is more difficult, ask anyone who has negotiated a long-term consulting contract where milestones are set in concrete, there is no lack of clarity or purpose. Or, in a merger or acquisition, there are always specifics that outline what happens next and what will change. When agreements seem like photo opportunities and there is "beautiful" progress, people will wonder why all the fuss. It's not done until it's done.

ALL OR NOTHING USUALLY MEANS NOTHING

- *Know when to hold 'em, know when to fold 'em.*

It's the ultimate ultimatum. It is also only the win or lose option without compromise. The world is not black or white. When a leader sets up the win or lose situation, he or she needs to be prepared to lose. If the situation is a loss, move on. It's better not to set it up this way because people will keep score of wins and losses. For a President dealing with sensitive diplomacy and complicated relationships, it is especially important to not set up the win/lose equation. As Donald Trump is learning, more likely the outcome is an ambiguous victory or nebulous defeat.

HOISTING THE DISTRESS FLAGS

- *Asking for help may be the strategy to move forward but can be seen as a sign of weakness.*

It is not a weakness to ask for help when in trouble. Leaders can do it too. It is not a sign of weakness. In fact, it is a sign of understanding one's limits and showing humility in order to get things done no matter what it takes. A leader who takes responsibility for his or her actions and explains them which sometimes may include asking for help is seen as a human. Autocrats don't ask for help. Bureaucrats ask for too much help and bog down any process or decision-making. Leaders ask for assistance when it is required and are appreciative when it is offered. Think of disasters and one leader asking another for help or offering help. It is a sign of good will and good leadership.

GRAY IS THE NEW BLACK...

- *An ambiguous victory is better than a nebulous defeat.*

Clarity is always the goal, but some issues are so complex that clear-cut victories are elusive. Nonetheless, the big issues need solving and sometimes progress is all that is required. As the progress develops, the opportunity to claim ambiguous victories is the best you might be able to do. Small changes in policy, executive orders, and elimination of silly regulations are all ambiguous victories.

ARE YOU WITH ME OR AGAINST ME?

- *Asking others to pick sides will guarantee conflict. Is there a middle?*

Lines drawn in the sand create drama, but they also create situations that can try a leader. Can we move the line later? Some situations faced by a leader are cut and dried, black or white. Most are not so clear. Picking sides leaves very little room for discussion but it does create fierce loyalty. A base of supporters who never waiver is a powerful force for any leader. It is the group that creates a base from which to operate. No one can ever claim Donald Trump doesn't have that base.

YOU CAN'T ALWAYS GET WHAT YOU WANT

- *Not all deals are economic deals. Treating all deals like a business deal will be seen as narrow minded and cold.*

Deals are complicated. There is give and take, there are details, there are misunderstandings, and they can be messy. Sometimes you make deals with yourself, "I am not going to drink alcohol in January". Sometimes you make deals with a spouse, "I will stay with you until your term is over". Sometimes you make deals with the devil, "I will do anything you say if I get elected". And sometimes there is no deal to be had. Deals are a key skill in leadership. It's just not all deals.

IT'S ALL ABOUT THE BENJAMIN'S

- *Taxes are to be paid. They will catch you, run you down, and make you wish you were never born.*

The perception of the IRS is of an army of hapless clerks wearing green eyeshades sitting behind desks arranged in long rows. At random, they plunk a hapless citizen from the stack and torture that citizen with threats. Think again. Although not privy to inside information, the IRS has secret powers and systems that find any of us who are foolish enough to fight with them. A leader who fights with the IRS is especially susceptible to punishment and ridicule. Selfish leaders use power for personal gain but the IRS doesn't care. Be honest and pay the IRS what is due.

12

The Summary

The story of Donald Trump and his leadership will be a source of debate, research, and discussion for the foreseeable future. He likes it that way. Leaders aspire to make change and he has changed things. History will tell in what direction.

OLD DOGS AND NEW TRICKS GIVE A CLUE

- *People don't change. The leader you know is the leader you get.*

We hope and pray people will change to be better, more likable, more effective, and more Presidential. Our hopes and prayers are rarely if ever answered. Leaders understand what got them there whether it be through hard work, family fortune, or good luck. Any promises made on accepting a new leadership role won't mean much as they return to the mean. Leaders are not different than any of us, we don't change. The Donald Trump you know is the Donald Trump you will get. Set expectations accordingly.

UNPRECEDENTED. THAT'S IT. THAT'S ALL.

- *If the intent is to leave a mark, you did it. If "unprecedented" was the descriptor.*

Looking back, that was quite a leadership ride. Great leaders accomplished things that were unprecedented. But despotic dictators and maniacal kings and queens did things also that were unprecedented. Donald Trump and his actions and style and behaviors can only be described as unprecedented. History will tell which side of the delicate unprecedented scale he will rest. Will it be the unprecedented for good or the unprecedented for not quite right?

Epilogue

As of this writing, Donald Trump is going through impeachment proceedings. A part of the inquiry is in regard to his leadership style. Is leadership style much in question? Whether he remains in office or not or whether he is reelected or not, his leadership style and day-to-day activities have changed the way we look at what leadership can mean. He has rewritten rules and broken glass on many tenets of leadership theory. I doubt he even knows or considers it. But time will tell the impact he has had on leadership. One thing I know, doing the right thing hasn't changed, the path to great results hasn't changed, and the critical role of the leader hasn't changed.

Index

A

AARP model, 35
"Acting" people, 68
Administration, Trump, 65, 75,
    85, 120
Admits mistakes, 149
Age limits for leaders, 147
"Agree in concept," 162
Air Force One, 148
Ambiguous victory, 163
"Analysis paralysis," 93
"Appropriate behavior," 2
Armstrong, Lance, 16

B

Banking regulation, elimination
    of, 38
BDT (Before Donald Trump), 50
"Beautiful" progress, 162
Behavior of Mr. Trump, 2
"Being crazy," accusations of, 130
Being current, 89
Belgium, 128
"Believe Me," 55
Best people, 66
Bigotry, symbol of, 21
Bond, James, 101
Booming economy, 96
Boorish behavior, 111
Brand
    positive agenda, 12
    power of, 145
    sign of, 21
Brand-new organization, 91

Breakfasts, 108
Brexit, 32
Broken record strategy, 54
Building security walls, 114
Bureaucracy, bypass lots of, 39
Bush, George W., 121, 159
Business Roundtable, 77
Business skills, 113, 131, 141

C

California fires, 109
Campaign, 7
Career, course of, 85
Caring about people, 26
Cash, Johnny, 160
Casual comments, 51
Celebrity, 24
Change, definition of, 33
Children crying, 126
Climate change, 42
Command and control
    management, 40
Communications strategy, 59
Communications tool, 49, 50
Community, 116
Competency perspective, 11
Complex issues, 41
Compliment, 150
Confidential information, 57
Consensus
    opposite of, 38
    process of, 112
Constant harassing, 43
Corporation management, 104
Counselors, 83

Credibility
    lying, enemy of, 6
    truth, telling the, 19
Crisis recovery, 106
Criticism, 10, 72, 75, 120, 126,
          150, 157

D

Dancing with the Stars
          (TV show), 151
Decision-making process, 22, 76,
          94, 163
Declaring victory, 111
Demeaning names, 150
Diplomatic victories, 13
Disaster, appropriate actions, 109
Discrimination, 145
Disloyalty, 88
Distractions, bombardment of, 37
Divisiveness, symbol of, 21
"Do No Harm," Google credo of, 122
Do-nothing leader, 31, 43
Don Quixote, 86
Doubt credibility, 27
Drug approvals, acceleration of, 38
Duck Dynasty, 15

E

Economic deals, 164
Ego, 144, 158
Einstein, Albert, 8
Emergency, case of, 132
Emotional outburst, 52
Emotion manage, 133
Empathy, 16, 19
Employee engagement, 40
Employee survey, 49
Empowerment, 40
Empty threats, 87
Environmental safety rules, 42

Equality, 16
Equipment require logistics, 41
European Union, 44
Exclamation points, 55
Execution, 29
Executive orders, 39
Experience, lack of, 31

F

Facebook, 101
Fashion accessory, 76
F-bomb, 52
Feedback systems, 73, 81
Floods in Houston, 109
Followers, number of, 15
Football game in Alabama, 78
Ford, Henry, 113
Foreign leader, "deal" with, 131
Foreign policy, 46, 65
Forrest Gump, 153
Forward progress, 120
Freedom of speech, 103
Frequent Flyer Miles, 15
Fresh perspective, 139
Future behavior, 115

G

Golf time, 58
Greenland, 128
Grove, Andy, 77
Guarantee conflict, 164

H

Handshake, symbol of power, 135
Healthy ego, 25, 144
Helter skelter, 37
Hitler, Adolph, 12
Homework/preparation, 92
"Horseplay," 84

"Huge, perfect, big, beautiful,"
    Trump description, 97
Humanity, 110

I

Iceland, 128
Immigration policy, 32, 44, 126
Impeachment, 47, 134
Important and attention, 22
Improve performance, 64
Inauguration ceremony, 47
Inclusive management style, 40
Independent investigations, 72
Ineffective leaders, 122
Inertia, 30
Information, watch television, 92
Innovative thing, 30
Intelligence community, 76
Interim, title of, 45
International diplomacy, 105
International travel, 148
Intervention, 130
Intimidation, 43
Iran Treaty crisis, 32
IRS, perception of, 165
Israeli embassy move, 46
Israeli issue, 32

J

Job growth, 13
Jobs, Steve, 8, 91
Jobs, Trump administration, 65
Judge Judy, 99
Judgment, 99, 116

K

Keeping records, 95
Killing agreements, 162
Knee-jerk reactions, 75

L

Large operations people, 41
Lawyers, 83, 115
Leader's apology, 109
Leaders command attention, 12
Leadership game, 111
Leadership Lessons from Attila the Hun, 141
Leadership skill, Trump
    decision making, 22
    likability surveys for, 35
    taken risks, 24
Leadership style, 12
Leadership theory, 3
Leadership thinking, 122, 124
Leader's legacy, 21
Leading from Behind, 141
Learning and development
    opportunity, 62
Legal opinion, 111
"Likability index," 35
Lincoln, Abraham, 60, 145, 158
Listening function, 89, 142
"Listening session," 110
"Lock her up," 17
Long-standing/pent-up problem, 38
Long-term allies and friends, 127
Loyalty, 79
Lying, enemy of credibility, 6

M

"Make America Great Again"
    vision, 17, 18, 21, 44
Man of the Year in 1938, 12
Meetings, storming out of, 143
Mexico, 128
Military actions and plans, 44
Military rebuilding, 38, 40
Misstatements of Donald Trump, 9
Moleskine notebooks, 95

N

National debt number, 22
Natural disasters, 106
Neeson, Liam, 101
Newman, Paul, 101
Nicknames, 20
9/11 victims, 103
Nixon, Richard, 74
The "No Asshole Rule," 144
Nonmilitary perspectives, 69
Nonsense vision, 44
Not quite right (NQR), 119
"No Whiners," 23
NQR. *See* Not quite right (NQR)
Nuance company, 60
Nuclear disarmament treaties, 37
Nuclear weapon policy, 73, 151
NY Times, 94

O

Obama, Barack, 159
Off-color jokes, 51
Offense, operating on, 74
Offensive symbols, 21
Off-handed comments, 51
Orange jumpsuit, threat of, 79
Organization chart matter, 65
Organization's success, 81

P

Pandora's box, 36
Paranoid survive, 77
Passive aggressive, 63
Patriotism, 116
Pay dividends, 129
Pay off people, 84
Peace agreements, 62
People care, 13, 46
People issues, 61

People thinking, 7
Performance reviews, 14, 73
Perks, critical/boast about, 143
"Permanent record," 123
Personal style and appearance, 98
Pinocchio nose, 5
Plain aggressive, 63
Plan, commitment to, 46
Plan matters, 44
"Planning time," 58
Plans and project management, 69
"Playing telephone" game, 57
Political organization, 41
Pornography, 117, 154
Positive track, US back on, 115
Predecessor, success formula, 121
Preparedness, 90
probation period, 14
Property, United States, 128
Protocols matter, 136
PTSD tendency, 76
Pushing people, 156

R

Racism, 100, 145
Racist jokes/comments, 51, 66
Real estate mogul, 90
Red baseball cap, 21
Reinvention activity, 35, 90
Relationships, 82, 126, 155
Resignation, sigh of, 43
Responsibility, 74, 163
Rules and regulations
        elimination, 34

S

Second-in-command, 86
Second opinion, 111
Secret code, Trump, 56
Self-awareness, 141, 144

"Send them back," 17
Sensitive diplomacy, 16, 162
Sexual in discussion, 117
"Sharpie" marker, 105
"Shiny objects," 36
"Shooting someone on
        5th Avenue," 16
Simpsons' TV, 20
Situations, complexity of, 41
Slavery, 100
Slogans, 17
Smart people around Trump, 152
Smile approach, 142
Social media, 97, 101, 139
Social skills, 93
Spacy, Kevin, 16
"Special assistant" role, 62
Speech, figures of, 23
Spokesperson, 59, 102
Spousal relationships, 82
Standards change, 146
Subpoena, receipt of, 115
Success, formula for, 121
Super Bowl champions, 136
Supporters, 16, 57
Surprise decisions, 75
Survival mode, 47

T

Teamster wisdom, 64
Terrorism, 19
Think of Kennedy, 21
Think of Nixon, 21
Thoughtful, 141
360-degree review, 81
Time Magazine, 12
Timing of tweet, 55
Toga parties, 93
Top-down management style, 40
"To tell you the truth," 23
Trade agreements, 105

Trade policy, 44
Trust, 11
Truth, telling the, 19
Turnover, high rate of, 67
Twitter, 50, 56

U

Understand issues, 92
Unemployment rate, 22, 56
"unfit," mental/emotional
        qualification, 73
"Unprecedented" Trump actions,
        8, 168
Unproductive activities, 110
Unraveling trade agreements, 44
Untruths tend, 25

V

Vengeful billionaire, 137
Vindictiveness, 17
Violence, threats of, 104
"Visible signs of progress" (VSOP),
        30
Vision matters, 44
VSOP. *See* "Visible signs of
        progress" (VSOP)

W

Washington, George, 124, 145
Wayne, John, 18
Willingness, 24, 27
Work, Trump effect at, 3
World Series baseball game, 78
World wars, 136
"WTF!" Leaders, 8

Y

"You're Fired!", 68

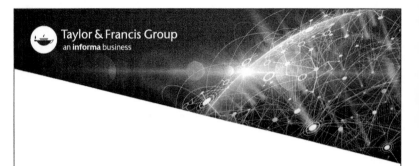